JANE HARPER

Less is More

Your Step-by-Step Guide to Overcoming Clutter and Chaos Forever

Copyright © 2024 by Jane Harper

All rights reserved. No part of this publication may be reproduced, stored or transmitted in any form or by any means, electronic, mechanical, photocopying, recording, scanning, or otherwise without written permission from the publisher. It is illegal to copy this book, post it to a website, or distribute it by any other means without permission.

Third edition

This book was professionally typeset on Reedsy.
Find out more at reedsy.com

Contents

Introduction	1
Chapter 1: The Philosophy of Minimalism	4
The Origins of Minimalism	4
Modern Minimalism	7
Chapter 2: The Benefits of Owning Less	10
Reducing Stress	10
Increasing Happiness	13
Chapter 3: Identifying What's Truly Important	16
Values Assessment	16
Prioritizing Essentials	19
Chapter 4: Decluttering Your Living Space	22
The KonMari Method	22
Room-by-Room Approach	25
Chapter 5: Minimalism in Digital Life	28
Digital Detox	28
Streamlining Digital Tools	31
Chapter 6: Financial Freedom Through Minimalism	34
Budgeting Basics	34
Investing in Experiences	37
Chapter 7: Minimalist Mindset	41
Mental and Emotional Clarity	41
Meditation and Mindfulness	44
Chapter 8: Minimalism for Families	47
Simplifying Family Life	47
Raising Minimalist Children	50
Chapter 9: Sustainable Living	52

Eco-Friendly Choices	52
Reducing Carbon Footprint	55
Chapter 10: Minimalism in Work and Productivity	58
Simplifying Task Management	58
Focusing on What Matters	61
Chapter 11: The Art of Saying No	65
Setting Boundaries	65
Prioritizing Self-C Care	68
Chapter 12: Maintaining a Minimalist Lifestyle	71
Continual Improvement	71
Embracing Change	74
Conclusion	76
Minimalism Resources and Tools	80
Minimalism Resources and Tools	81

Introduction

Welcome to a journey toward a more fulfilling, less cluttered life. This book is for anyone who's ever felt overwhelmed by the sheer volume of things they own or the pace of their daily routine. The goal here isn't just to clear out your closet or tidy up your living room; it's to fundamentally change your relationship with your possessions and your surroundings.

Minimalism is often misunderstood. It's not about stripping away all of life's pleasures or living in stark emptiness. Instead, it's about making intentional choices that align with your values and aspirations. When you own less, you create more space for joy, creativity, and meaningful experiences.

In today's fast-paced world, we're encouraged to accumulate more and more — more items, more commitments, more responsibilities. Before we know it, we find ourselves buried under a mountain of "stuff" and wondering why we feel so stressed and unhappy. This book invites you to pause, reassess, and embark on a path to simplicity.

Embracing minimalism isn't about deprivation; it's about enrichment. Picture your ideal day. Are you rushing around from task to task, or are you spending time on activities and with people that truly matter to you? By focusing on what's genuinely important, you'll find that you can lead a richer, more satisfying life.

So, what can you expect from this book? Each chapter is carefully designed to guide you through a different aspect of minimalism. You'll learn not just what minimalism is, but why it matters and how to practically integrate it into every facet of your life.

We'll start with the philosophy of minimalism, digging deep into its origins and how it has evolved in modern times. Understanding the "why" behind minimalism sets a strong foundation for the changes you'll make. We'll then move on to explore the many benefits of owning less, such as reducing stress and increasing happiness. Minimalism isn't a one-size-fits-all; it's a personal journey that varies for everyone.

Following that, we'll get hands-on with practical strategies, like assessing your values and prioritizing essentials. You'll learn how to declutter your living space using methods that ensure you keep only what sparks joy. And it's not just about your physical space—your digital life deserves a makeover too. We'll explore strategies for decluttering your digital world, from reducing screen time to organizing your digital files.

Next, we'll delve into financial freedom through minimalism, guiding you on budgeting basics and how to invest more in experiences rather than material goods. This chapter will help you see that financial minimalism can lead to more financial security and peace of mind.

We'll also address the critical role of mindset in maintaining a minimalist lifestyle. Mental and emotional clarity, mindfulness, and meditation can support your minimalist journey, helping you stay grounded and focused on what truly matters.

If you have a family, you'll find tailored advice in the chapter on minimalism for families. Simplifying family life and teaching children about the value of less can create a harmonious and cohesive household environment. It's never too early to start instilling these values.

Sustainability is another vital aspect of minimalism, and we'll cover how making eco-friendly choices and reducing your carbon footprint can align perfectly with a minimalist lifestyle. A simpler life is often a greener one, creating benefits not just for you but for the planet as a whole.

Productivity isn't left behind either. Learn how to simplify your task management and focus on what truly matters in your professional life. Less clutter in your workspace often translates to a clearer mind and more efficient work habits.

And then there's the art of saying no—an important yet often neglected

INTRODUCTION

aspect of minimalism. Setting boundaries and prioritizing self-care are essential skills that help you maintain your newfound lifestyle.

Finally, maintaining a minimalist lifestyle requires continual improvement and a willingness to embrace change. This isn't a one-time project but a lifelong commitment to living with intention.

By the end of this book, you'll have the tools, knowledge, and inspiration to transform your life. Minimalism is a path to freedom. Freedom from the anxiety of too many possessions, from the tyranny of overloaded schedules, and from the pressure to keep up with an unsustainable pace of life.

Whether you're just curious or ready for a significant lifestyle overhaul, this book will meet you where you are. The benefits of minimalism are profound and multifaceted, affecting everything from your home and finances to your mental well-being and relationships.

So, let's embark on this journey together. By choosing to own less and live more intentionally, you'll not only create a space that serves and inspires you but also carve out a life filled with purpose and joy. Welcome to the start of your minimalist journey.

Chapter 1: The Philosophy of Minimalism

In a world overflowing with material goods and endless distractions, the philosophy of minimalism offers a refreshing change, inviting you to strip away the unnecessary to focus on what truly matters. Embracing minimalism is less about counting possessions and more about creating space—both physical and mental—for a richer, more purposeful life. This journey isn't about deprivation but about clarity and intent, allowing you to align your environment with your values. By actively choosing simplicity, you free yourself from the weight of excess and make room for joy, meaningful experiences, and genuine connections. It's a deliberate dance between necessity and desire, where each step towards less unlocks a world of more—more peace, more freedom, and more fulfillment. In understanding minimalism's core principles, you'll uncover a path not just to live with less but to live more fully, embracing a lifestyle that's both sustainable and profoundly liberating.

The Origins of Minimalism

Tracing the origins of minimalism brings us to a rich tapestry of cultural and philosophical roots. Minimalism as a concept isn't a modern invention. It has historical precedents that stretch back to ancient civilizations that valued simplicity and intentionality. While each culture had its unique interpretation, the central theme has always been about reducing excess to focus on what truly matters.

One of the earliest references to minimalist philosophy can be found in ancient Eastern traditions, particularly within Zen Buddhism. Zen monks practiced asceticism, which emphasized the importance of living with only the bare essentials. The aim wasn't just to own less but to cultivate a heightened state of awareness and mindfulness. Everything they did, from tea ceremonies to art, focused on simplicity and clarity.

In the West, the ancient Greeks also had their own version of minimalism. Stoic philosophers like Epictetus and Seneca advocated for a life of virtue and wisdom over one of material excess. According to Stoicism, contentment comes from within, not from external possessions. They believed that by limiting our desires and focusing on personal growth, we could achieve greater happiness and peace of mind.

Fast forward to the 19th century, and one cannot overlook the influence of Henry David Thoreau. His experiment in simple living at Walden Pond has been a touchstone for modern minimalist thinking. Thoreau's observations about the burdens of materialism and the virtues of simplicity continue to resonate with those seeking a pared-down lifestyle. His famous quote, "Simplify, simplify," encapsulates the essence of minimalist philosophy.

In the world of art and design, minimalism made a significant impact in the 20th century. Artists like Donald Judd and architects like Ludwig Mies van der Rohe brought the ethos of "less is more" into the realm of visual arts and architecture. Their works stripped away unnecessary elements to highlight form and function, influencing everything from furniture design to urban development.

As we progressed into the late 20th and early 21st centuries, minimalism began to crystallize as a lifestyle choice rather than just an artistic or philosophical concept. The pressures of consumerism and the fast-paced, cluttered nature of modern life made the minimalist approach increasingly appealing. Inspirational figures like Joshua Fields Millburn and Ryan Nicodemus, who founded "The Minimalists" movement, have brought minimalism into mainstream consciousness. Through their books, podcasts, and films, they advocate for a life with fewer possessions but richer experiences.

Additionally, the convergence of technology and minimalism presents a fascinating chapter in its evolution. With the advent of the digital age, the inundation of information and digital clutter became new areas where minimalism could be applied. Techniques like digital detoxing and decluttering digital spaces have become integral aspects of modern minimalism.

So, why has minimalism endured across different cultures and epochs? It's likely because, at its core, minimalism addresses some of the most essential human needs: the desire for peace, clarity, and genuine happiness. It calls us to focus on our values, to purge the superfluous, and to live more intentionally.

Perhaps the beauty of minimalism lies in its adaptability. It's a philosophy that doesn't prescribe a one-size-fits-all solution. Whether influenced by Zen monks, Stoic philosophers, or modern advocates, the central tenet remains—less can indeed be more. As we navigate through the complexities of today's world, the origins of minimalism remind us that simplicity, intentionality, and mindfulness are timeless keys to a fulfilled life.

The journey into minimalism may seem daunting at first, especially in a society that equates success with accumulation. However, a closer look at its origins shows us that striving for less has always been about achieving more—not in the material sense, but in terms of well-being, satisfaction, and clarity. This historical perspective gives us a robust framework to understand how minimalism can be applied to various aspects of our lives, encouraging us to strip away the nonessential to reveal what truly makes us happy.

Now that we understand where minimalism comes from, it becomes easier to see its relevance in our lives. We aren't just adopting a trend; we are embracing a philosophy that's deeply embedded in human history, offering wisdom that transcends time and culture. At its best, minimalism isn't about deprivation; it's about empowerment. It's about freeing ourselves from the unnecessary so we can devote our energy to what genuinely enriches our lives.

Next, we'll delve into how modern minimalism has evolved to meet our contemporary challenges, making it even more pertinent for today's fast-paced, cluttered world. But before we do, let's take a moment to appreciate the rich heritage that has shaped this transformative philosophy. It's a reminder that in seeking less, we often find far more than we ever imagined.

CHAPTER 1: THE PHILOSOPHY OF MINIMALISM

Modern Minimalism

Stepping into the realm of modern minimalism, we're greeted with a philosophy that's both timeless and timely. At its core, modern minimalism is about making intentional choices—choices that lead to a life filled with purpose and clarity rather than clutter and chaos. While the idea of minimalism has ancient roots, today's take on it reflects our unique challenges and opportunities in the 21st century.

Technology, for instance, has brought both convenience and complexity into our lives. We're constantly bombarded with information, notifications, and digital "noise." Modern minimalism encourages us to filter out this noise, focusing instead on what's truly necessary and valuable. This means curating not just our physical spaces, but also our digital environments.

Minimalist home designs often showcase clean lines, neutral colors, and open spaces that breathe. But modern minimalism isn't just about aesthetics; it's about function. The furniture you choose, the gadgets you keep, and even the art on your walls—everything should serve a purpose or bring joy. This is reminiscent of William Morris' famous directive: "Have nothing in your houses that you do not know to be useful, or believe to be beautiful."

Consider your wardrobe. Capsule wardrobes, a modern minimalist trend, are a testament to the power of fewer yet better choices. By carefully selecting versatile, high-quality pieces, you free up mental space, reduce decision fatigue, and help the environment by consuming less. This approach can extend beyond clothes to other areas, such as skincare routines, kitchen gadgets, and even your social calendar.

But modern minimalism isn't just about deprivation or Spartan living; it's about abundance—an abundance of time, mental space, and meaningful experiences. When you let go of excess belongings and commitments, you make room for the things that truly matter. This can lead to increased happiness and reduced stress, two important benefits we'll explore further in the next chapter.

In a world that's constantly urging us to upgrade, buy more, and hustle harder, modern minimalism offers a refreshing counter-narrative. It's about recognizing that more isn't necessarily better. By embracing this mindset, you align your life more closely with your values, focusing on depth rather than breadth.

Another aspect of modern minimalism is the emphasis on sustainability. By owning and consuming less, you significantly reduce your carbon footprint. This includes making eco-friendly choices like buying second-hand, opting for products with minimal packaging, and supporting companies that prioritize sustainability. This conscious consumption creates a ripple effect, influencing those around you and contributing to a healthier planet.

Modern minimalism also invites us to reconsider how we spend our time. Are your days filled with busyness but lacking in meaning? By eliminating unnecessary tasks and commitments, you create space for what truly enriches your life. This could be quality time with loved ones, pursuing a passion project, or simply enjoying moments of solitude.

One of the most compelling aspects of modern minimalism is its flexibility. There's no one-size-fits-all approach. What works for one person might not work for another, and that's okay. The key is to find a balance that suits your lifestyle and aligns with your values. Whether it's reducing physical clutter, simplifying your schedule, or focusing on sustainable living, the principles of modern minimalism can be adapted to fit your unique circumstances.

It's also worth noting that modern minimalism doesn't mean never buying anything new or refusing all modern conveniences. Rather, it's about being deliberate with your choices. It's asking yourself whether a new item will genuinely add value to your life or whether it's merely a fleeting desire created by external pressures.

For families, modern minimalism offers a different kind of richness. It encourages creating environments where children learn to value experiences over possessions. By simplifying family life, you teach your children the joy of creativity, the value of relationships, and the importance of sustainability. These lessons can have a lasting impact, shaping their attitudes and behaviors for years to come.

In the workplace, modern minimalism can enhance productivity and job satisfaction. A clutter-free desk and a pared-down to-do list can lead to

CHAPTER 1: THE PHILOSOPHY OF MINIMALISM

greater focus and efficiency. It encourages prioritizing tasks that have a significant impact, rather than getting bogged down with busywork. This streamlined approach can help you achieve better work-life balance, reducing stress and increasing fulfillment.

Ultimately, modern minimalism is a tool for creating a life of purpose and joy. It challenges us to thoughtfully consider what we let into our homes, our minds, and our hearts. By doing so, we can craft a simpler yet richer existence, free from the excesses that weigh us down.

As you embark on your journey towards modern minimalism, remember that it's a personal and evolving process. It's about making incremental changes that lead to lasting transformation. You don't have to overhaul your life overnight. Start small, be patient with yourself, and celebrate each step you take toward a more minimal and meaningful life.

The beauty of modern minimalism lies in its potential to enhance every aspect of your life. From your home and digital spaces to your relationships and personal growth, adopting minimalist principles can lead to profound and rewarding changes. Embrace the philosophy of less is more, and you'll find that in reducing the extraneous, you make room for the truly extraordinary.

Next, we will delve into the tangible benefits of owning less. You'll discover how reducing physical and mental clutter can lead to a life of greater happiness and reduced stress. The journey to a minimalist lifestyle is filled with challenges and rewards, but through each step, you'll find yourself closer to a life of greater clarity and joy.

Chapter 2: The Benefits of Owning Less

Living a life with fewer possessions does more than just clear out your space; it transforms your entire existence. Imagine waking up each morning to a home that feels light and open, where every item has a purpose and adds value to your life. The simple act of owning less can significantly reduce stress, allowing you to breathe easier and focus on what truly matters. Additionally, the shift to minimalism can pave the way for increased happiness, as you begin to invest more time and energy into experiences and relationships rather than material goods. You'll find that letting go of the non-essentials creates room for joy, creativity, and a newfound sense of freedom. By embracing this lifestyle, you're not just decluttering your home; you're creating a more meaningful and fulfilling life. So, get ready to explore the uplifting benefits of owning less and watch as your well-being soars to new heights.

Reducing Stress

In today's fast-paced world, stress often feels inevitable. We juggle work, family, and personal commitments, continually adding more to our plates. However, when we shift our focus from accumulation to elimination, a profound transformation begins. Owning fewer possessions can significantly reduce stress, offering mental clarity and emotional relief that many of us desperately seek.

Stress is closely linked to the clutter in our lives—both physical and mental. Studies have shown that cluttered spaces can lead to heightened levels of cortisol, the stress hormone. The more items we accumulate, the more our minds feel overwhelmed and chaotic. By reducing the number of things we own, we create an environment that is conducive to peace and tranquility. Imagine coming home to a space free of unnecessary clutter; a place where everything has a purpose and a place. This kind of environment can become a sanctuary, a refuge from the external pressures of life.

Minimalism doesn't just clear physical spaces; it also clears mental spaces. When our homes are streamlined, our minds follow suit. Decision-making becomes easier without the noise of excess. Each item in our living space serves a purpose, eliminating the cognitive burden of too many choices. This principle applies to many aspects of life, from wardrobe choices to kitchen gadgets, and even to our social calendars. Simplification inherently reduces the stress associated with decision fatigue.

Moreover, managing fewer possessions means less time spent on maintenance and cleaning. Consider the hours you spend tidying up, organizing, and cleaning your home. When you own less, these tasks become significantly simpler. This reclaimed time can be invested in activities that bring joy and relaxation, further reducing stress levels. A minimalist life doesn't demand that we sacrifice comfort or aesthetic pleasure; rather, it invites us to relish in the simplicity of having exactly what we need and nothing more.

Financial stress is another significant component that many of us face. Owning more often means spending more money—not just on the initial purchase but also on upkeep and storage. By embracing minimalism, we shift our financial priorities. Instead of buying multiple low-quality items, we invest in fewer, high-quality pieces that are more durable and bring more satisfaction. This approach not only reduces the stress of dealing with frequent replacements but also brings financial stability.

Minimalism can also transform how we spend our time. A cluttered home often leads to a cluttered schedule, filled with activities and responsibilities that don't truly matter. By owning less and prioritizing what really matters, we find more time to engage in activities that nurture our well-being. This might mean having more time to exercise, pursue a hobby, or simply unwind without the pressure of endless to-do lists. The result? A significant reduction in the stress that comes from feeling perpetually busy but never productive.

Relationships, too, can benefit from a minimalist approach. When we own fewer possessions, we may find ourselves placing greater value on experiences and connections rather than material goods. This shift can lead to deeper, more meaningful interactions with our loved ones. The time we previously spent on managing and organizing our stuff can be redirected to nurturing these relationships, bringing joy and reducing the stress that often accompanies social engagements driven by obligation rather than genuine desire.

Additionally, minimalist living can enhance our relationship with ourselves. By stripping away the extraneous, we can better understand what truly matters to us. This self-awareness can lead to greater emotional clarity and stability. We no longer use possessions to fill emotional voids or to signify our worth. Instead, we find contentment in who we are, not what we own. This profound sense of self can be incredibly liberating and stress-relieving.

Let's not forget the impact technology and digital clutter have on our stress levels. Owning less extends to our digital life as well. By minimizing digital distractions, such as reducing apps, limiting social media use, and decluttering our online spaces, we can free ourselves from the constant notifications and information overload that contribute to stress. A more intentional digital presence allows us to focus better and feel more at ease.

There's also a social aspect to consider. Societal pressures often push us towards owning more—keeping up with the latest trends or seeking validation through material possessions. Choosing minimalism can be a radical act of defiance against these societal norms. It's a declaration that our worth isn't tied to the things we own. This mindset shift can alleviate the stress that comes from societal expectations, granting us the freedom to live authentically and on our own terms.

Implementing a minimalist approach might initially seem daunting, especially in a world that prizes consumerism. However, the incremental steps toward reducing possessions can be incredibly rewarding. Start small—focus on a single drawer or a specific category of items. The process is as much about the journey as it is about the destination. Each item you choose to let go of brings you closer to a life of reduced stress and greater fulfillment.

Minimalism is not a one-size-fits-all solution. It's about finding what works for you, discovering the balance that brings peace and reduces stress in your unique life. Whether it's decluttering your wardrobe, simplifying your kitchen, or even choosing to live in a smaller home, each step towards owning less is a step towards a more serene existence. The ultimate goal isn't just a clean, organized space; it's the mental and emotional clarity that comes from it.

In conclusion, owning less has profound benefits for reducing stress. By eliminating physical clutter, we create peaceful environments that reflect our true values. Financial stability, enhanced relationships, and better use of our time are natural byproducts of this lifestyle. As we navigate the journey towards minimalism, we find that the simplest, most meaningful life is well within our reach. The calm that comes from living with less is not just an external change but a deeply internal one, paving the way for a truly fulfilling life.

Increasing Happiness

Simplicity carries a powerful promise: increased happiness. When you own less, your life gets lighter, less cluttered, and filled with more joy. But how does reducing material possessions translate into genuine happiness? It's a multifaceted transformation that begins in the space around you, extends into your mental landscape, and affects every aspect of your life.

Imagine waking up in a room that's clean, uncluttered, and filled with only the things that add value to your life. Instead of feeling overwhelmed by the sheer amount of stuff, you're likely to feel a sense of calm and clarity. You know where everything is, and more importantly, you know why it's there. Each item has a purpose and sparks joy. This seemingly simple change helps to reduce decision fatigue, a silent stressor in our daily lives.

Additionally, owning fewer things can lead to financial stability. When you aren't constantly buying new items, you save money that can then be used for meaningful experiences or saved for future security. Financial stress is one of the most common causes of unhappiness. Liberating yourself from the need to acquire more can provide peace of mind and a sense of freedom.

Moreover, reducing possessions shifts focus from material objects to personal relationships and experiences. Instead of spending weekends shopping, you might find joy in spending quality time with loved ones, embarking on small adventures, or simply enjoying quiet moments in nature. Social connections and experiences often bring more lasting happiness compared to fleeting joy derived from material things.

One of the most profound ways owning less increases happiness is through the cultivation of gratitude. When you have fewer things, you appreciate them more. Each item takes on more significance, and you learn to value quality over quantity. This shift in perspective fosters a mindset of thankfulness which, according to research, is a key component of a happy life.

Mental well-being improves as well. Clutter often triggers anxiety and stress. Conversely, a well-organized space promotes a peaceful mind. It becomes easier to practice mindfulness, to be present in the moment, and to engage in deep, meaningful activities. Your living environment supports mental clarity, paving the way for a more serene state of being.

And let's not overlook emotional health. Being surrounded by unnecessary items can create a sense of being trapped or overwhelmed. By eliminating what you don't need, you make room for introspection and emotional growth. You begin to understand what truly matters to you, which in turn gives your life a clearer direction and purpose.

The journey toward owning less also teaches valuable skills like decision-making and problem-solving. When you choose to keep only the essentials, you must determine what's truly important. This habit spills over into other areas of life, making you a more decisive and focused individual. The freedom of not being bogged down by excess allows you to devote time and energy to pursuits that genuinely enhance your happiness.

Consider the concept of "flow," a state in which you're fully immersed in activities that challenge yet engage you. With physical and mental clutter minimized, it's easier to enter this zone. Whether you find flow in creative projects, work, or hobbies, you'll often see that happiness naturally follows.

Furthermore, minimalism encourages you to live intentionally. Each choice, from what you buy to how you spend your time, becomes more deliberate. This intentionality leads to a more meaningful and fulfilled life. You're no longer passively accepting whatever comes your way but actively shaping your existence based on values and priorities.

The benefits multiply over time. Initially, you might experience simple relief from decluttering your home. But as you dive deeper into the minimalist lifestyle, you notice broader, more impactful changes. Your relationships improve, your focus sharpens, and your daily experiences feel richer and more satisfying. These changes build on one another, creating a virtuous cycle of increasing happiness.

Community bonds often grow as well. Living with less encourages a sense of community and sharing. Instead of owning every possible tool or gadget, neighbors and friends can lend and borrow items, fostering a sense of connection and mutual support. These social interactions play a crucial role in enhancing well-being and satisfaction with life.

Minimalism doesn't mean you have to become a monk with a single robe and bowl. It's about making deliberate, thoughtful choices that align with your values and contribute to your well-being. It's a personal and unique journey, tailored to your life and needs, and when you strike that perfect balance, the happiness you uncover is profound and enduring.

Lastly, remember that the process is ongoing. It's not about reaching a final, pristine state but about continually making choices that maximize happiness and minimize stress. As your life evolves, so will your understanding of what truly brings you joy. Embrace change, and let your minimalist path adapt accordingly. By doing so, you're investing in long-term happiness, fostering a life rich in purpose and fulfillment.

In summary, owning less is not just about reducing clutter. It's about creating a lifestyle that enhances your happiness. It's about living intentionally, saving money, appreciating what you have, and fostering better relationships. The journey might start small, but the happiness gained is profound and long-lasting. Embrace minimalism, and let it lead you to a happier, more meaningful life.

Chapter 3: Identifying What's Truly Important

As we journey further into minimalism, it's crucial to differentiate between what we think we need and what genuinely matters. Identifying what's truly important begins with a deep dive into your core values. It means aligning your time, energy, and possessions with your inner beliefs. Often, we cling to items or commitments out of habit or societal pressure, but minimalism invites us to strip back these layers. Ask yourself what brings you joy and purpose, and you'll often find it's not material things, but experiences and relationships that hold true value. When you prioritize essentials over excess, you'll start seeing a shift—not just in your surroundings, but in your emotional well-being. It's about living a life intentionally curated to reflect who you really are and what you genuinely value. With a clarified focus, every aspect of your life can become more meaningful and fulfilling.

Values Assessment

To embark on the journey of minimalism, it's essential first to understand our values. This isn't just about listing what we like or value superficially, but diving deep into our core beliefs and what truly matters most in our lives. Values assessment is the cornerstone of identifying what's genuinely important to us, paving the way to a life of clarity and intention.

Begin by asking yourself what brings you joy and fulfillment. Think about

CHAPTER 3: IDENTIFYING WHAT'S TRULY IMPORTANT

the moments that have left a lasting impression on you, the activities that make you lose track of time, and the relationships that enrich your life. Contemplating these experiences can offer valuable insights into your core values.

Sometimes, what we think we value differs from what we actually do. It's easy to get caught up in the daily grind, focusing on short-term goals and gratifying wants. But once we dig deeper, we realize that certain pursuits and possessions aren't as significant as we believed. This process often involves a bit of soul-searching, and yes, it can be uncomfortable. But discomfort is a powerful tool for transformation.

Consider these guiding questions for your values assessment:

- What activities or experiences make you feel most alive and content?
- Who are the people in your life that you cherish the most, and why?
- When have you felt the most proud of yourself?
- What are the causes or ideals you deeply care about?
- What would you like to be remembered for?

Take your time with these questions. Write down your thoughts, and don't rush the process. This isn't a test with a time limit but an opportunity to explore your inner world. The answers might surprise you, and that's a good thing. Clarity often comes from prolonged introspection and honesty.

Sometimes, it helps to categorize your values. For example, you might realize that family comes first, followed by health, personal growth, and then financial stability. These categories can act as a framework to prioritize your life and help you make decisions aligned with your values.

It's crucial to distinguish between intrinsic values and extrinsic aspirations. Intrinsic values are things that are genuinely important to you, such as relationships, personal achievements, and well-being. Extrinsic aspirations often revolve around material possessions, social status, and outward appearances. While there's nothing wrong with wanting nice things, placing too much importance on them can detract from a more meaningful existence.

Here's a practical exercise:

1. Write down a list of everything you currently spend your time on, including work, hobbies, social activities, and chores.
2. Next to each activity, note how much time you spend on it weekly.
3. Now, rate each activity on a scale of 1 to 5 on how aligned it is with your core values.

You'll likely find a significant gap between some of your activities and your values. This gap represents room for change, where you can cut back on things that don't truly matter and focus more on what genuinely enriches your life.

Many find it helpful to visualize their values by creating a vision board or a journal. Keep reminders of your core values visible in your daily life; it could be a note on your mirror, an inspiring quote as your phone's wallpaper, or a dedicated page in your planner. These small prompts can reinforce your commitment to living aligned with your values.

When you evaluate your values, it's also important to consider the role that consumerism has played in shaping your priorities. Society often promotes the accumulation of goods as a measure of success and happiness. However, if striving for the next big purchase has led to stress and dissatisfaction, it's time to reassess.

Think back to any significant purchases you've made recently and ask yourself: Did they provide lasting fulfillment, or were they momentary fixes that soon faded into the background? Minimalism challenges us to rethink our relationship with material possessions and seek contentment from experiences and relationships instead.

As you start aligning your life with your values, you'll likely face resistance, both internally and externally. It's natural to feel attached to familiar routines and possessions, and you might also encounter pushback from those around you who don't understand your new path. Remember that this is a personal journey, and it's okay if others don't immediately see the value in your choices. Consistency will speak volumes over time.

Another aspect of values assessment is regularly revisiting and refining your values. Life is dynamic, and as you grow, your priorities may evolve. It's healthy and necessary to periodically reflect and make adjustments. Schedule time every few months to review your values list and see if it still holds true. This practice ensures that you remain on a path that resonates deeply with your current self.

In conclusion, values assessment is an ongoing, introspective process that forms the foundation of a minimalist lifestyle. By identifying and living in alignment with your core values, you create a life filled with purpose and joy. You strip away the unessential, leaving more room for what truly matters. Embracing this practice not only simplifies your existence but also enhances your overall well-being, leading to a richer, more fulfilling life.

Prioritizing Essentials

In the pursuit of minimalism, the first step to success is identifying what truly matters in our lives. Without a clear understanding of what's essential, any effort to declutter, simplify, or streamline can feel aimless and unfulfilling. This process isn't about stripping away joy or comfort but rather about making room for it by eliminating the superfluous. Let's explore how to prioritize those essentials effectively.

To begin, reflect on your core values. What are the non-negotiable aspects of your life that bring you joy, fulfillment, and a sense of purpose? These could be relationships, passions, health, or personal growth. Identifying and acknowledging these values creates a solid foundation upon which to base your decisions. Our lives often become bogged down with tasks, possessions, and commitments that don't align with our true selves. By focusing on our values, we detoxify our lives of these unnecessary elements.

Next, it's crucial to differentiate between needs and wants. Needs are those things that are indispensable to our well-being, while wants can enrich our lives but are not essential. By honing in on our needs, we can trim the excess that's often rooted in societal pressures and consumerist culture. For example, you might realize you need eight hours of sleep for optimal health but don't necessarily need the latest tech gadget that's been causing you financial stress.

One practical method for identifying what's essential is the "Four Burners Theory." Imagine your life is represented by a stove with four burners: family, friends, work, and health. To be highly successful in one area, you may need to turn down the others. Decide which burners need to be on high heat and which ones can simmer. Make deliberate choices about where to focus your energy.

It's also useful to conduct a periodic audit of your activities and commitments. Most of us carry a mental load of "shoulds"—things we think we should be doing but that don't actually add value to our lives. Are there activities or commitments you've outgrown or that don't serve you anymore? Perhaps you're investing hours in unpaid overtime while neglecting self-care or passions that bring you joy. Letting go of these extraneous activities can be profoundly liberating.

Setting boundaries is another significant step in prioritizing essentials. It's often easier said than done, especially if you're a people-pleaser or if you're used to saying yes to every request. Learning to say no without guilt can help you reclaim your time and focus on what truly matters. Start small by setting boundaries around your time for yourself before expanding to other areas of life.

Mindfulness practices can also be incredibly helpful in discerning what's essential. Techniques like meditation, journaling, or even a quiet walk can serve as opportunities for deep introspection. By giving yourself the space to think without distractions, you can gain clarity about what should hold a place in your life and what should be let go.

Remember, prioritizing essentials isn't a one-time task but an ongoing process. As you evolve, so too will your understanding of what's important. Life stages, career changes, and even personal losses can shift your priorities dramatically. Allow yourself to regularly reassess and adjust your focus to stay aligned with your evolving values and needs.

Making physical space for what's important is another key step. This means decluttering in a way that aligns with your prioritized essentials. If family dinners are important, but your dining table is buried under a mountain of papers, you're not setting yourself up for success. Creating environments that support your priorities can make it easier to live according to your values.

Invest in quality over quantity. This doesn't just pertain to physical objects but also to your time and relationships. Strong, deep connections with a few individuals are often more fulfilling than superficial connections with many. The same goes for activities—deeply investing in a few interests rather than spreading yourself thin over many can lead to greater satisfaction and achievement.

Lastly, embrace simplicity in communication and relationships. Practice directness and honesty, so your connections are meaningful and free from misunderstandings or unnecessary complexity. Clear, straightforward communication can minimize misunderstandings and reduce emotional clutter, making room for more authentic and supportive relationships.

Prioritizing essentials isn't about deprivation; it's about liberation. By focusing on what truly matters, you open up space—not just in your physical environment but in your mental and emotional realms as well. This newfound space helps reduce stress, increases happiness, and allows you to live a life more aligned with your true self. It's a continuous journey, but a deeply rewarding one.

Chapter 4: Decluttering Your Living Space

Creating a serene and organized living space is more than just tidying up—it's about paving the way for a lifestyle that brings both clarity and joy. This chapter is designed to guide you through the transformative process of decluttering, where you'll let go of physical items that no longer serve a purpose in your life. As you begin this journey, focus on what sparks joy, simplifies your daily routine, and aligns with your true values. By methodically assessing each item and dedicating time to tackle each room, you'll discover the immense freedom and peace that comes with owning less. Remember, it's not about perfection but about progress and the gradual creation of a space that nurtures your well-being and inner peace. As you move forward, take it one step at a time and celebrate the small victories along the way, knowing that each one brings you closer to a more meaningful and fulfilling life.

The KonMari Method

The KonMari Method, pioneered by Marie Kondo, has revolutionized the way people approach decluttering. This method isn't about mere cleaning; it's a transformative process that allows individuals to create a living space that aligns with their values and enhances their well-being. Rooted in the belief that our surroundings directly affect our inner state, the KonMari Method emphasizes mindfulness, introspection, and the joy of living with less.

At its core, the KonMari Method encourages you to ask a simple yet profound question: "Does this item spark joy?" This question serves as the guiding

CHAPTER 4: DECLUTTERING YOUR LIVING SPACE

principle for deciding what to keep and what to let go of. It's not just about practicality or utility; it's about emotional resonance. Holding each item in your hands and evaluating its impact on your feelings cultivates a deeper awareness of what truly matters to you.

The process begins with envisioning your ideal lifestyle. Rather than diving straight into the physical act of decluttering, take a moment to visualize what you want your life and home to look like. How do you want to feel in your space? What activities do you want it to support? This vision becomes your compass, guiding you through the decluttering journey with a clear sense of purpose and intention.

The KonMari Method follows a specific order, which is designed to help you build momentum and hone your decision-making skills. You start with categories, not rooms, and proceed in this sequence: clothes, books, papers, komono (miscellaneous items), and finally, sentimental items. This progression from easier-to-tackle items to more emotionally charged possessions makes the process manageable and less overwhelming.

Sorting through your possessions category by category allows you to see the full extent of what you own. When you gather all your clothes in one place, for instance, the sheer volume might be eye-opening. This visual impact serves as a wake-up call, prompting you to reconsider your consumption habits and the importance you place on material goods.

As you handle each item, pay attention to your physical and emotional reactions. An item that sparks joy will often elicit a feeling of happiness, warmth, or excitement. Conversely, items that don't spark joy might make you feel anxious, guilty, or indifferent. Trust these feelings—they're invaluable in guiding your decisions.

It's crucial to approach this process with gratitude. Expressing thanks to items before letting them go acknowledges their role in your life and allows you to part with them on a positive note. This practice not only eases the emotional difficulty of decluttering but also instills a deeper appreciation for the things you choose to keep.

Once you've decided what to keep, the next step is to find a designated place for each item. Storage should be simple, yet practical, maximizing both accessibility and aesthetics. The KonMari Method favors vertical storage, where items are stored upright rather than stacked. This technique not only saves space but also allows you to see everything at a glance, which can be incredibly satisfying.

A key aspect of the KonMari Method is its emphasis on respect and care for your belongings. Fold your clothes with intention, organize your books in a way that honors their role in your life, and treat your living space as a sanctuary. This mindfulness fosters a closer relationship with your possessions and a more harmonious living environment.

Undoubtedly, one of the most profound aspects of the KonMari Method is its ripple effect. As you declutter your physical space, you may find that other areas of your life begin to transform as well. Many people report experiencing greater mental clarity, improved decision-making, and a newfound ability to focus on what truly matters. In essence, the order you create externally can lead to a deeper sense of peace and contentment internally.

Remember, the KonMari Method is not about achieving perfection. It's about fostering an environment that supports your well-being and brings you joy. Take your time with the process and be compassionate with yourself. Decluttering can be emotionally and physically taxing, so it's essential to proceed at a pace that feels right for you.

By the time you complete the KonMari Method, your living space will reflect a more intentional and meaningful life. You'll be surrounded by items that resonate with your values and contribute to your happiness. In this way, decluttering becomes not just a one-time event, but a valuable skill that you can carry into all aspects of your minimalist journey.

Embrace the KonMari Method as more than just a cleaning technique—see it as a powerful tool for self-discovery and transformation. As you peel away the layers of excess, you'll uncover a lifestyle that's simpler, more fulfilling, and more aligned with your true self. And in doing so, you'll pave the way for a life that not only looks better but feels better, too.

CHAPTER 4: DECLUTTERING YOUR LIVING SPACE

Room-by-Room Approach

The journey to a clutter-free and more intentional living space begins with a clear plan. Tackling your home room by room not only makes the monumental task more manageable but also allows you to experience a series of small successes that motivate you to keep going. So, let's roll up our sleeves and dive into each area with strategies designed to help you lead a simpler, more meaningful life.

The Entryway

Start with the entryway, as it's the first area you and your guests see upon entering your home. Often, this space becomes a drop zone for shoes, bags, and miscellaneous items. Begin by sorting through everything and only keep what you need. Consider installing hooks for keys and a small bench with storage for shoes. A clean entryway sets the tone for the rest of your home.

The Living Room

The living room is where many of us spend a significant portion of our time, relaxing and entertaining. It can also become a repository for various items. Start with the largest pieces of furniture and work your way down to smaller items. Assess each piece: Does it bring joy or serve a purpose? If not, it's time to let it go. Clear out shelves, coffee tables, and entertainment centers. Be ruthless with DVDs, books, and knick-knacks. Remember, less is more.

Consider investing in multifunctional furniture like a sofa bed or an ottoman with hidden storage. This not only saves space but also reduces clutter. As you clear away excess, leave only items that truly enhance your living experience.

The Kitchen

The kitchen is often the heart of the home but can quickly become one of the most cluttered rooms. Start by emptying out your cabinets and drawers. Sort items into piles: keep, donate, and toss. Be realistic about what you need. Do you really need three spatulas or five mismatched coffee mugs? Stick to the essentials and items that bring you joy when cooking or eating.

Group similar items together and think about accessibility. Frequently used items should be within easy reach. Store bulkier, seldom-used appliances like the turkey roaster in less accessible areas. Consider clear, labeled containers for pantry items. A streamlined kitchen not only looks better but also makes meal preparation more enjoyable.

The Bedroom

Your bedroom should be a sanctuary, a peaceful retreat from the outside world. Start with your wardrobe. Use the "one-year rule": if you haven't worn it in the past year, it's time to say goodbye. Donate or sell clothes that are still in good condition, and discard anything worn out or beyond repair. Focus on keeping versatile, quality pieces that you love.

Move on to other areas like nightstands, dressers, and under the bed. Clear out any items that don't contribute to a restful environment. Consider minimalist décor to create a calming atmosphere. Store away seasonal items and keep surface areas clear of clutter.

The Bathroom

A clutter-free bathroom is both calming and functional. Go through your toiletries and discard expired or unused items. Keep only what you use daily. Utilize drawer organizers or small baskets to keep items like makeup, hair products, and toiletries sorted and easily accessible.

Consider installing shelves or a medicine cabinet for additional storage if space allows. Less clutter on your counters often translates to a quicker, smoother morning routine. Remember, the goal is to create a space that supports your well-being.

The Home Office

If you have a home office, you know how quickly paperwork and office supplies can accumulate. Start with your desk, clearing off everything and only putting back the essentials: your computer, a good lamp, and a few select items. File important documents and shred anything you no longer need. Use storage solutions like files, baskets, or digital storage to keep papers organized.

For office supplies, keep only what you use regularly and find homes for the rest. A tidy, organized office space can significantly boost your productivity and mental clarity.

The Laundry Room

Laundry rooms can easily become a clutter magnet. Start by clearing out all shelves and cupboards. Discard old cleaning supplies or lost socks that no longer serve a purpose. Organize what's left into functional categories: detergents, fabric softeners, and ironing supplies.

If space allows, install shelves or a cabinet to keep items off surfaces, creating a more organized look. Simple changes like designated hampers for each type of laundry can streamline your routine and make the space more efficient.

The Garage

The garage is often the most daunting space to declutter. Start with one section at a time and be methodical. Create zones for different categories: tools, sports equipment, seasonal décor, etc. Use shelving, hooks, and pegboards to keep everything off the floor and easy to find.

If you haven't used an item in the past year—be it a tool, a piece of garden equipment, or an old bicycle—consider donating it. A well-organized garage can free up space for activities and make your belongings more accessible.

This room-by-room approach helps break down the overwhelming task of decluttering into manageable steps.

By focusing on one area at a time, you can see immediate results, motivating you to continue. Create a home that supports your well-being, comfort, and happiness, one room at a time. With patience and persistence, you'll find that a decluttered space brings with it a sense of calm and clarity, setting the stage for a minimalist lifestyle that truly resonates with your values and desires.

Chapter 5: Minimalism in Digital Life

In our hyper-connected world, it's easy to get overwhelmed by the constant barrage of notifications, emails, and social media updates. Embracing minimalism in your digital life means making conscious choices to reduce digital clutter and focus on what's truly important. Start by conducting a digital detox—identify apps, subscriptions, and even devices that don't add value to your life, and let them go. Streamlining your digital tools not only helps reclaim your time, but also enhances your mental clarity. Simplifying your online presence and workflows can create a more serene and productive digital environment, allowing you to be present and fully engaged in meaningful activities.

Digital Detox

In today's hyper-connected world, the concept of a digital detox might seem quaint, even rebellious. But what if I told you that it's a critical component to a minimalist digital life? We find ourselves inundated with notifications, emails, and social media updates, so much so that our phones have become extensions of ourselves. This constant connectivity contributes to an overwhelming sense of urgency and anxiety, pulling us away from not just our goals but our very sense of well-being. The idea of a digital detox is not simply about unplugging; it's about re-centering and finding balance.

Why should we undertake a digital detox? For starters, digital clutter can be just as mentally exhausting as physical clutter. The numerous apps, endless notifications, and unending streams of information create a mental noise that

CHAPTER 5: MINIMALISM IN DIGITAL LIFE

is hard to escape. This constant bombardment leads to stress and reduces our capacity for mindfulness, creativity, and deep work. By selectively pruning our digital environments, we can create space for more meaningful activities that genuinely enrich our lives.

Consider starting small. Begin by identifying the most intrusive aspects of your digital life. Is it incessant email notifications? Is it the mindless scrolling through social media feeds? Is it the incessant ping of messages? Pinpoint these areas and set specific times of the day to handle them. Creating these boundaries can be incredibly liberating. Imagine the tranquility of a morning spent in mindfulness, or the joy of an evening truly engaged with your family, free from the digital world's demands.

To begin your digital detox journey, consider these essential steps:

1. **Audit Your Digital Life**: Take an honest inventory of all digital devices and platforms you use regularly. Note how often you use them and for what purposes. This step will help you understand where your digital influx comes from and identify obvious areas for reduction.
2. **Set Clear Intentions**: Ask yourself what you aim to achieve with a digital detox. Is it to regain focus, reduce stress, or reclaim time for other activities? Your reason will guide your actions and help you stay committed.
3. **Establish Tech-Free Zones and Times**: Dedicate certain areas of your home and specific times of the day as tech-free. It could be your dining table, bedroom, or a couple of hours before bed. These boundaries create predictable sanctuaries from digital interruptions.
4. **Curate Your Digital Environment**: Unsubscribe from newsletters, delete seldom-used apps, and unfriend or unfollow accounts that don't bring you joy or value. Curate your digital spaces just as you would a treasured room in your home.

Another practical step is to embrace the use of tools and settings that help enforce your digital detox. Many smartphones and apps now come with features that allow you to monitor screen time, set limits on certain apps, or schedule periods where notifications are paused. Leveraging these tools can provide a framework that supports your objectives.

Remember, this process is about progress, not perfection. There will be days when you find yourself slipping back into old habits, and that's perfectly okay. The key is to be mindful of these moments and gently nudge yourself back towards your goals. It's also helpful to replace the time spent on digital devices with more enriching activities, like reading a good book, going for a walk, or engaging in a hobby you love.

The impact of a digital detox extends beyond individual well-being; it ripples out, improving our relationships, productivity, and even creativity. When you free yourself from the constant digital chatter, you open up space for deeper connections with those around you. You become more present in conversations, more attuned to others' needs, and more capable of authentic interactions.

For those seeking a simpler, more meaningful lifestyle, the role of a digital detox can't be overstated. It's a necessary step in downsizing our lives to upsize our happiness. As we shed the excess, we make room for what truly matters, tapping into a richer, more fulfilling existence.

It's worth mentioning that a digital detox is not just a one-time event but an ongoing practice. Regularly scheduled digital detoxes, whether they are weekly, monthly, or quarterly, can serve as a reset button for your mind and spirit. These pauses give you the opportunity to recalibrate, assess what is working, and make necessary adjustments.

As you embrace this digital detox, the initial discomfort will give way to newfound freedoms. Your mind will feel less cluttered, your attention more focused, and your spirit rejuvenated. Embrace this journey with an open heart and a willing spirit, for the rewards are immense and far-reaching.

- **Increase Mindful Moments**: Mindfulness is often lost in our multitasking digital lives. By reducing digital engagement, we create more moments to practice mindfulness, leading to greater mental clarity and emotional resilience.
- **Boost Productivity**: Limits on digital distractions invariably lead to

increased productivity. You'll find yourself completing tasks more efficiently and with greater focus when you're not constantly interrupted by notifications.
- **Enhance Real-Life Connections**: Disconnecting from the digital world opens opportunities to connect in real life. Quality time with loved ones becomes more meaningful when devices are set aside. You'll quickly notice the depth of relationships grow.

In some ways, undertaking a digital detox is an act of reclaiming your own time and space. It's a form of self-care that allows you to be more intentional about how you spend your time. You become the curator of your own life, choosing what gets your attention based on your values and priorities, rather than the demands of endless notifications and messages.

Finally, let's remember that a digital detox is not about completely abandoning technology. It's about calibrating your relationship with it to ensure that it serves your life rather than dictates it. As with all things in minimalism, the balance lies in intentionality, purpose, and alignment with your true values.

Streamlining Digital Tools

In the hustle and bustle of today's hyper-connected world, digital tools can either be a boon or a bane. The allure of countless apps and tools promises greater efficiency and productivity, yet often the result turns out to be digital clutter. To truly embrace minimalism in digital life, it's crucial to streamline the tools we use. By consciously choosing and organizing digital tools, you not only reclaim mental space but also foster a more intentional, and ultimately more fulfilling, relationship with technology.

Take a moment to assess the digital tools you're currently using. Do you have multiple apps serving the same purpose? Are there tools you signed up for, only to forget they exist? Identifying redundancy is the first step toward digital minimalism. Keep it simple and opt for one app per category whenever possible. For instance, if you have three different note-taking apps, challenge yourself to pick just one. Often, the simplest tool can meet most, if not all, of your needs.

Next, consider the tools that genuinely add value to your life. Just because a tool is new or popular doesn't mean it's right for you. Reflect on your daily activities and goals—does this application help you achieve these in a meaningful way? If the answer is no, it's time for it to go. Remember, every tool you use should be a conscious choice, not an automatic addition.

Organizing your digital tools is an ongoing process. Start with your home screen and desktop. They should be clean and intuitive. Create folders with meaningful labels to group similar apps together. This might seem like a trivial task but believe me, it makes a significant difference in how often and how efficiently you use those tools.

It's not just about the tools themselves but also about how you use them. Implement practices that support minimalism. For example, consider using cloud storage to avoid file redundancy and keep your devices clutter-free. Develop a habit of regularly reviewing and deleting unnecessary files and apps.

Now, let's talk about notifications—the disruptors of focus. While notifications can be useful, they can also drain your attention reserves. Turn off non-essential notifications to minimize interruptions. You don't need a ping every time someone likes your post or sends an email. Customize your settings to alert you only to the most critical updates.

Emphasizing quality over quantity also applies to your digital tools. Choose robust, multifunctional apps over multiple single-function apps. Multifunctional tools not only reduce clutter but also streamline your workflow. For example, a comprehensive project management tool can integrate tasks, calendars, and notes, negating the need for separate apps for each function.

Being mindful of your tool's usage patterns can also be enlightening. Use app tracking features to monitor the time spent on each tool. Are the hours spent on social media apps proportionate to their benefits? These insights can help you make better decisions about which tools to keep and which ones to discard.

Consider incorporating digital wellness tools that promote a healthy relationship with technology. Applications like screen time trackers can provide valuable insights into your tech habits. Utilizing these tools can help you become more aware of how much time you spend on unproductive activities and take steps to reclaim that time for what truly matters to you.

While you're streamlining your tools, don't forget about data management. Digital minimalism isn't just about the apps you use; it's also about how you handle your digital footprint. Regularly clean out your email inbox, old files, and unused applications. Use tools that help automate this process, providing regular purges so you don't have to think about it constantly.

The goal isn't to live a tech-free life but to foster a balanced digital ecosystem that serves your higher purpose. Less is truly more when it comes to digital tools. By thoughtfully curating and maintaining the apps and devices in your life, you can transform your digital space from a source of chaos into one of clarity and purpose.

Finally, don't hesitate to revisit and adjust your digital toolset periodically. Life evolves, and so do technology needs. Staying flexible and open to change ensures that your digital tools continue to support and enhance your minimalist lifestyle.

In your journey to streamline digital tools, you'll find that the real value lies in what you gain by shedding the excess: more focus, more intention, and more satisfaction. By curating a minimalist digital life, you're not just decluttering your devices; you're making room for a richer, more intentional existence.

Chapter 6: Financial Freedom Through Minimalism

Discovering financial freedom through minimalism means more than just trimming expenses; it's about aligning your spending with your values, living intentionally, and finding joy in experiences over possessions. By adopting a minimalist approach, you can create a life where finances no longer dictate your choices. Imagine the liberation of being debt-free, having a robust savings account, and the ability to invest in experiences that enrich your life and bring true happiness. Minimalism allows you to strip away the excess, revealing a clearer path to achieving your financial goals without the burden of unnecessary materialism. This journey towards financial independence does not just lead to a fatter wallet but offers peace of mind, reduced stress, and a newfound sense of control over your life. Whether it's through mindful budgeting or choosing to spend on experiences rather than things, minimalism provides the tools to craft a more purposeful, financially liberated existence.

Budgeting Basics

Financial independence and minimalism often go hand in hand. One starts with decluttering their physical space and the other, their financial life. Both endeavors lead to a greater sense of freedom and well-being. Budgeting might not be an exciting topic for most people, but it's essential for those looking to live a fulfilling minimalist lifestyle. Understanding how to allocate your money

CHAPTER 6: FINANCIAL FREEDOM THROUGH MINIMALISM

thoughtfully ensures that every dollar spent aligns with your true priorities.

First and foremost, budgeting begins with awareness. Sometimes, we don't realize how much we are spending until we meticulously document every expense. Start by tracking your income and expenses. This doesn't need to be a painful or tedious process. All it takes is a simple spreadsheet or one of the many budgeting apps available. By understanding where your money is going, you gain insights into areas you can cut back. This is the first step to financial freedom.

One of the principles of minimalism is intentionality, and this directly applies to budgeting. Prioritize spending that aligns with your values and long-term goals. When you purchase items or services, ask yourself if they serve a real purpose or add meaningful value to your life. This mindset change might save you more money than you expect over time. For instance, those morning lattes might seem insignificant, but they add up. Consider brewing coffee at home instead, which can be both cost-effective and rewarding.

Creating a minimalist budget doesn't mean you should be frugal to the point of deprivation. Rather, it's about making conscious choices. Distinguish between needs and wants. Essentials such as housing, utilities, groceries, and healthcare should always be a priority. However, think critically about discretionary spending. Do you really need a new gadget when your current one works just fine? Could that money be better spent on an experience or saved for future security?

To truly embrace the essence of a minimalist budget, simplify your financial obligations. Eliminate unnecessary subscriptions and memberships. A gym membership might seem like a necessity, but if you're not using it regularly, it's just an expense. Opt for home workouts instead. The same goes for streaming services or magazine subscriptions—only keep what you regularly use and enjoy.

Set clear and tangible financial goals. Whether it's paying off debt, saving for a future expense, or building an emergency fund, having defined objectives helps you stay focused and motivated. Minimalism supports this by encouraging you to cut out the fluff and direct your resources towards what genuinely matters.

Another critical aspect of budgeting basics is developing an emergency fund. Life is unpredictable, and having three to six months' worth of living expenses stashed away in a savings account can offer peace of mind. This safety net allows you to handle unexpected events without derailing your financial plans or plunging into debt.

Debt reduction is another cornerstone of minimalism in finances. Carrying debt often adds stress and ties you to financial obligations that limit your freedom. Aim to pay off high-interest debt as quickly as possible. Strategies such as the snowball method—paying off the smallest debts first to build momentum—or the avalanche method—focusing on high-interest debts— can be effective. The goal is to unshackle yourself from debt so you can redirect your money towards fulfilling and enriching experiences.

We can't ignore the importance of saving and investing in the conversation about budgeting. Allocate a portion of your income to savings and investments before you spend on non-essentials. This might mean automating transfers to a savings account or brokerage account right after payday. Over time, these small, consistent contributions can grow significantly due to the power of compound interest.

When it comes to investing, align your choices with minimalist principles. Seek out investment opportunities that promise growth without unnecessary complexity. Options like index funds and ETFs offer diversified exposure without the need for constant management, aligning well with a simplified financial strategy. Remember, the aim of minimalism is to simplify your life, not to burden it with intricate financial instruments.

Adopting a minimalist approach to budgeting also means embracing a flexible mindset. Life changes and so do financial needs and priorities. Regularly review and adjust your budget to reflect new circumstances or changes in income. Flexibility ensures that your budgeting aligns with your present reality, helping you stay on track without undue stress or rigidity.

Consider the benefits of financial minimalism on your overall well-being. Simplifying your finances reduces anxiety and stress, freeing up mental and emotional energy for more rewarding pursuits. You might find yourself with more time and peace of mind to focus on hobbies, relationships, and self-care.

This holistic effect underscores the interconnectedness of minimalism in all aspects of life, including finances.

Ultimately, budgeting basics under a minimalist philosophy pave the way for financial freedom and overall happiness. It's about being mindful and deliberate with your resources, ensuring they serve a purpose aligned with your core values and long-term aspirations. You don't have to be perfect, but consistency and intentionality will get you far.

By integrating these budgeting basics into your practice of minimalism, you're not just managing your money, but you're also cultivating a life that's rich in purpose and meaning. The path to financial freedom and greater happiness lies in simplicity and thoughtful management of your resources. By living below your means, aligning spending with your values, and continually adapting to changing circumstances, you can achieve a sense of control and well-being that transcends mere monetary wealth.

Investing in Experiences

When we talk about financial freedom through minimalism, it's crucial to challenge the traditional notion that wealth equals the accumulation of material goods. One of the most revolutionary changes we can make is to shift our spending from things to experiences. Why is this so powerful? Because experiences create memories, foster relationships, and cultivate personal growth, all of which outlast and outperform the fleeting joy of material possessions.

Material possessions often come with hidden costs. There's the obvious financial burden, but also the time and energy spent maintaining, organizing, and worrying about them. Experiences, on the other hand, offer a different kind of return on investment. When you spend money on experiences, you typically engage with others, explore new environments, and create stories that become an indelible part of who you are.

Research supports this idea. Studies have shown that people who spend money on experiences rather than material goods report higher levels of satisfaction and happiness. This is because experiences often involve anticipation, which can be a source of joy in itself. When you book a trip or plan a special outing, you have something to look forward to, which lifts your spirits long before the event even takes place.

Moreover, experiences often have a social component that amplifies their value. Sharing a meal with friends, attending a concert, or embarking on an adventure with loved ones can strengthen bonds and deepen relationships. Such interactions are rich in emotional content, providing a sense of connection and community that material possessions can't replicate.

Consider the investment of time and money into a cooking class instead of buying a new kitchen gadget. The skills and memories you gain from learning to cook a new cuisine will last far longer than the joy derived from another appliance cluttering your counter. Plus, you get the added benefits of healthier eating and perhaps even a new social activity if you go with friends or make new ones in the class.

This isn't to say that all material possessions are devoid of value. The key is to be mindful of what truly enhances your life and what merely adds to the clutter. You might invest in a good pair of hiking boots, but the ultimate joy and value come from the hiking experiences you have wearing those boots.

Minimalism encourages us to scrutinize our spending habits and align them with our core values. If financial freedom is a goal, then spending intentionally on experiences that uplift and fulfill you is a wise strategy. This approach minimizes regrets because experiences can't be easily replaced. They are unique to the time and place in which they happen, and often their mere recollection can bring joy.

It's also worth noting that experiences can foster a mindset of gratitude and contentment. When you reflect on a memorable trip, a delightful evening out, or a challenging but rewarding project, you're reminded of the richness of life beyond material accumulations. Such reflections can shift your focus from what you lack to what you already have.

Let's talk about practical ways to begin investing in experiences rather than things. Start by reallocating your budget. If you currently have a significant portion of your disposable income earmarked for shopping or upgrading gadgets, consider diverting some of that money into a "Experiences Fund."

This simple step can make a huge difference in how you utilize your financial resources.

Planning is vital. Look at your calendar and make conscious efforts to include activities that excite and inspire you. Whether it's a weekend getaway, a cooking workshop, or a day at the museum, putting these experiences on your schedule ensures they happen rather than remain as mere intentions.

Sometimes, the most fulfilling experiences are free or low-cost. A day hike, a visit to a local park, or even attending a free lecture can offer immense satisfaction without breaking the bank. The goal is to actively seek out enriching activities that resonate with your values and interests.

Families, too, can benefit from this shift in focus. Instead of showering children with toys and gadgets, parents can invest in family trips, memberships to zoos or museums, and even simple at-home activities like cooking meals together or game nights. These shared experiences create a strong family bond and memories that outlast any toy.

One significant advantage of investing in experiences is their potential to make you more adaptable and resilient. When you expose yourself to new environments and situations, you learn to navigate uncertainties and develop a broader perspective. These skills are invaluable and often lead to personal and professional growth.

Taking up new hobbies or learning new skills can also be incredibly rewarding. Whether it's picking up a musical instrument, learning a new language, or dabbling in photography, these experiences enrich your life, provide creative outlets, and often teach patience and perseverance.

At the community level, investing in experiences can enhance your social circle and bring about a sense of belonging. Joining local clubs, volunteering, or participating in community events can connect you with like-minded individuals and create a support network that no material possession can offer.

There are emotional benefits as well. Engaging in experiences that align with your passions and interests can provide a deep sense of fulfillment and purpose. They allow you to express yourself authentically and often lead to moments of profound joy and peace.

It's also essential to balance spontaneity with planning. Some of the best experiences happen unexpectedly. Leave room in your life for impromptu adventures and spontaneous activities that can often lead to surprisingly joyful outcomes.

To sum up, investing in experiences rather than material goods is a cornerstone of achieving financial freedom through minimalism. This shift allows you to live a richer, more fulfilling life while also providing the emotional and psychological rewards that material possessions can't offer. As you embrace this approach, you'll likely find yourself happier, more connected, and ultimately, more at peace.

Chapter 7: Minimalist Mindset

Embracing a minimalist mindset goes beyond merely decluttering your space; it's about transforming your mental and emotional landscape to align with the principles of simplicity. As you strip away the non-essential, you're given the opportunity to focus on what genuinely matters, leading to both mental and emotional clarity. Imagine liberating your mind from the chaos of everyday distractions and instead, channeling your energy toward more meaningful pursuits. This internal shift creates a fertile ground for mindfulness and meditation practices, allowing you to live with purpose and intention. Remember, adopting a minimalist mindset is not an overnight transformation, but rather a continuous, rewarding journey towards a life rich in experiences and free from unnecessary burdens.

Mental and Emotional Clarity

When we talk about the minimalist mindset, much of the focus tends to be on the physical—getting rid of items, organizing our homes, and so forth. But what about the mental clutter that can be equally, if not more, overwhelming? Mental and emotional clarity is the cornerstone of a minimalist lifestyle. It's about freeing up mental space in much the same way you would clear out a cluttered drawer. When your mind is uncluttered, you suddenly have room to focus on what truly matters, leading to a more fulfilling, purposeful life.

Most people are carrying around a huge mental load without even realizing it. Thoughts about work, personal relationships, financial worries, and everyday chores can become entangled in our minds, creating a chaotic environment that's hard to navigate. By adopting a minimalist mindset, we strive to untangle this web, simplifying our thoughts and emotions to achieve a sense of peace.

One effective method for achieving mental clarity involves regularly setting aside time for self-reflection. You don't need to pen a novel every evening; starting with just ten minutes a day can make a world of difference. Use this time to jot down your thoughts in a journal or to practice mindful meditation. Reflecting on your day, your emotions, and your goals can help identify areas where mental clutter is gathering. This simple practice can reveal much about what's weighing you down and offer insights into how to lighten the load.

Another powerful tool for mental clarity is practicing gratitude. Gratitude shifts your focus from what you lack to what you have. When your mind is constantly in a state of wanting or comparison, it's difficult to feel emotionally balanced. But by taking a few moments each day to acknowledge what you are thankful for, you shift your mindset from scarcity to abundance, fostering a sense of emotional well-being.

It's important to remember that mental clutter often stems from our environment. If your living space is chaotic, it's likely that your mind will mimic that chaos. To that end, start with the spaces where you spend the most time, like your bedroom or office. Simplifying these areas can provide a sanctuary of calm that can positively impact your mental state.

Decluttering doesn't mean you have to throw everything out. It means creating an environment that serves you, rather than stifles you. In the same way, mental decluttering means letting go of thoughts and emotions that do not serve your well-being. For example, letting go of past regrets or future anxieties can free up immense mental space.

Think about the relationships in your life. Are some of them more draining than fulfilling? It's not about cutting people off, but about setting healthy boundaries and prioritizing connections that uplift you. Emotional clarity often comes from nurturing positive relationships and minimizing toxic ones. This might mean having difficult conversations or even letting go of certain relationships for your mental peace.

Mindfulness practices can also aid greatly in mental clarity. Mindfulness is the act of being present in the moment, non-judgmentally. This simply means paying attention to your thoughts and feelings without getting caught up in them. By practicing mindfulness, you can become more aware of mental clutter as it arises and address it before it accumulates.

For instance, the next time you find yourself overwhelmed with thoughts or emotions, take a moment to pause. Focus on your breathing, acknowledge what you're feeling, and then gently guide your mind back to the present. This practice not only reduces stress but also builds emotional resilience over time.

Another key element in mental and emotional clarity is learning to let go of perfectionism. Let's face it: Perfection doesn't exist. Constantly striving for a flawless life adds unnecessary mental clutter and stress. Embrace the concept of "good enough." When you accept that things don't have to be perfect, you alleviate a significant amount of mental stress, making room for what's truly important.

Additionally, a minimalist mindset encourages a focus on what truly matters, which often involves identifying your core values. For mental and emotional clarity, it's vital to understand what's non-negotiable in your life. What are the things you absolutely value and cannot compromise on? When you identify these, it's easier to align your thoughts, feelings, and actions accordingly. This alignment reduces mental conflict and creates a clear path for emotional clarity.

Remember that maintaining mental and emotional clarity is an ongoing process. It requires consistent effort and self-awareness. Begin by taking small steps and gradually make these practices a part of your daily routine. It's about progress, not perfection. As you continue on this journey, you'll start to notice subtle yet significant changes in your mental and emotional well-being.

In conclusion, mental and emotional clarity isn't about achieving a constant state of Zen; it's about creating mental space to focus on what's genuinely important. By incorporating practices like self-reflection, gratitude, mindfulness, and setting boundaries, you begin to declutter your mind and emotions. This clarity not only enhances your happiness but also allows you to live a more intentional, meaningful life. Embrace the minimalist mindset to reclaim your mental and emotional well-being, setting a strong foundation for a life filled with purpose and joy.

Meditation and Mindfulness

When seeking a simpler, more meaningful life, harnessing the power of meditation and mindfulness can be transformative. In a world bombarded by stimuli and ceaseless chatter, these practices offer a sanctuary of calm, promoting mental clarity and emotional stability. Through meditation and mindfulness, one cultivates a deeper awareness of the present moment, letting go of unnecessary stress and focusing on what truly matters.

Imagine starting your day with a few moments of quiet reflection, focusing on your breath and centering your thoughts. This simple practice can set the tone for the day, equipping you with a composed and balanced mindset that helps you navigate daily challenges with grace. When the mind is clear, decisions come easier, and the clutter in your life—both physical and mental—can be addressed with newfound clarity.

Meditation is often perceived as a daunting endeavor that requires a specific setting or an extended period. However, it can be as simple as sitting quietly for a few minutes and paying attention to your breathing. The key is not the duration but the consistency and intention behind the practice. Start with five minutes each morning, creating a routine that becomes a non-negotiable part of your day. As you become more comfortable, you can gradually extend the time, reaping greater benefits.

Additionally, mindfulness isn't restricted to a seated meditation practice. It can be woven into the fabric of daily life, bringing awareness and presence to mundane tasks. Whether you're washing dishes, taking a walk, or even folding laundry, mindfulness transforms these activities into moments of peace and clarity. Mindfulness teaches us to appreciate the simplicity and beauty of each moment, channeling our focus away from material distractions.

Let's delve into the practical aspects. Start by creating a quiet space in your home, free from distractions. This doesn't have to be an entire room—just a small, uncluttered corner dedicated to your practice. Make it inviting by adding elements that encourage relaxation, such as a cushion, a soft blanket, or a plant. Consistency in location helps signal to your brain that it's time to settle into a calming routine.

Guided meditation apps can also be an excellent resource for beginners, offering a structured path to develop your practice. Many of these apps provide short, approachable sessions designed to fit into a busy schedule. Over time, as you become more attuned to your practice, you may find that you don't need the guidance as much and can meditate independently. This shift often signifies a deeper connection with your inner self and growing comfort in silence.

Integrating mindfulness into your minimalist mindset also involves learning to be present during moments of decision-making. For instance, when choosing to purchase a new item, pause and ask yourself: "Do I really need this? Will it add value to my life?" By being present and mindful, you can make conscious decisions aligned with your minimalist values, reducing impulsive buys and subsequent clutter.

Let's not forget about emotional clarity. Our emotions often drive our actions, leading to unnecessary complications and stress. Regular mindfulness practice allows for emotional regulation, helping you acknowledge and process emotions without judgment. This increased awareness enables you to respond to situations with intentionality rather than react impulsively. Over time, you'll notice a significant reduction in anxiety and an increase in emotional resilience.

In the realm of work and productivity, meditation and mindfulness can be a game-changer. Clear, focused minds perform better and are less likely to be overwhelmed by multitasking and stress. Implementing brief meditation breaks throughout the workday can refresh your mental state and improve productivity. Consider setting a timer to remind yourself to pause, take deep breaths, and recalibrate your focus.

However, remember that the goal of these practices isn't perfection but progress. You may encounter days where your mind is restless or you skip your meditation session. It's crucial to approach these instances with compassion and understanding, rather than self-criticism. The journey to mindfulness is ongoing, and each step, no matter how small, contributes to your overall well-being.

Meditation and mindfulness are more than just stress-relief techniques—they are essential components of a minimalist mindset. They guide us toward a life less cluttered by material possessions and more enriched by meaningful experiences and deep connections. As you embrace these practices, you'll discover the profound impact they have on your perspective, helping you prioritize what truly matters and live with intention.

To sustain these benefits, make meditation and mindfulness an integral part of your minimalist lifestyle. Reflect regularly on your progress, celebrate small victories, and remain adaptable. Life will continue to present challenges, but with a grounded practice, you'll navigate them with greater ease and grace. As you continue this journey, remember that the essence of minimalism lies not in the absence of material items, but in the richness of a life well-lived.

Chapter 8: Minimalism for Families

Incorporating minimalism into family life might feel like navigating through chaos, but it can be a deeply rewarding journey toward a more meaningful and stress-free existence. It's about creating an environment where every family member understands and values simplicity. Begin with open conversations to align everyone's expectations and introduce changes gradually, fostering a supportive atmosphere. Simplify routines, prioritize quality time, and declutter communal spaces, making room for shared experiences over possessions. As you implement these principles, observe the profound impact on your family's well-being, creating a home filled with purpose and joy. Each small step taken together will build a stronger, more connected family unit.

Simplifying Family Life

We often hear the phrase "family life is chaotic" and accept it as a universal truth, but what if it doesn't have to be that way? The principles of minimalism offer a refreshing approach to creating a serene, joyful, and more meaningful family life. Stripping away the non-essentials helps focus on what truly matters – togetherness, growth, and mutual support. Let's explore how a minimalist lifestyle can simplify family life and foster a deeper connection among family members.

First and foremost, embracing minimalism as a family requires a united vision. When everyone is on board, the transition is smoother and more meaningful. Start by having an open discussion about what minimalism means to each family member. Talk about the benefits, share your personal motivations, and set shared goals. This will not only align everyone's efforts but also strengthen family bonds as you work towards a common objective.

One of the cornerstones of simplifying family life is decluttering shared spaces. Begin with communal areas like the living room, dining room, and kitchen. These are the hubs of family interaction and can quickly become cluttered with toys, papers, and miscellaneous items. By minimizing possessions in these areas, you create a more welcoming, peaceful environment where family members can connect without the distractions of excess. Aim for furniture and decor that serve a functional purpose, and encourage each family member to actively participate in keeping these spaces tidy.

Meal times can also benefit immensely from a minimalist approach. Start by simplifying your meal planning and cooking routines. Opt for nutritious, simple meals that are easy to prepare and bring joy to the table. Create a weekly meal plan that everyone can contribute to and look forward to. This not only reduces the stress associated with meal times but also ensures that everyone eats healthier, home-cooked meals more consistently. An added bonus is the opportunity to involve children in cooking, fostering early skills and a sense of responsibility.

Speaking of children, raising them in a minimalist environment doesn't mean depriving them of joy or experiences. It means choosing experiences over possessions and teaching them the value of quality over quantity. Instead of inundating your children with an overwhelming amount of toys and gadgets, curate a selection of high-quality, versatile items that encourage creativity and prolonged engagement. This way, children learn to appreciate and take care of their belongings, understanding that less can indeed be more.

Daily routines and schedules are another area ripe for minimalism. Streamlining daily tasks can significantly reduce stress and create more time for meaningful activities. Analyze your family's daily schedule and identify areas where you can cut down on obligations. Perhaps you're stretched thin with extracurricular activities, leaving little room for family time. Prioritize activities that add real value to your family's life and aren't just filling up time slots. Let go of the rest, and you'll find that your days have more breathing

CHAPTER 8: MINIMALISM FOR FAMILIES

room for intentional, shared moments.

Minimalism also plays a crucial role in managing family finances. Financial stability is a cornerstone of a peaceful home life. Together, examine your family's spending habits and set shared financial goals. Simplify budgeting by categorizing and prioritizing spending, focusing on necessities and meaningful experiences over material possessions. This collective approach to managing money not only reduces financial stress but also sets a positive example for children about mindful spending and saving.

The benefits of minimalism extend to family relationships as well. When the external noise is reduced, communication can flourish. Make it a practice to have regular family meetings where everyone can share their thoughts, feelings, and suggestions without distractions. This openness strengthens familial bonds and ensures everyone feels heard and valued. Encourage active listening and empathy during these sessions, fostering an environment of mutual respect and understanding.

Moreover, a minimalist lifestyle encourages the practice of gratitude, an essential component of a fulfilling family life. Regularly take time to reflect on and appreciate the simple joys of family togetherness. Develop small rituals of gratitude that involve all family members, such as sharing one thing you're thankful for during dinner. This simple act shifts focus from what's lacking to the abundance of love and support that surrounds you.

As you navigate the journey towards a simplified family life, remember that the process is equally as important as the outcome. Minimalism is not a one-time project but an ongoing commitment to living more intentionally. Begin with small, manageable changes and gradually build them into the fabric of your family life. Celebrate your progress and be patient with the gradual nature of transformation.

In conclusion, simplifying family life through minimalism involves more than just reducing physical clutter. It's about fostering genuine connections, creating meaningful routines, and instilling values that will benefit every family member in the long run. The objective is to cultivate a home environment that supports happiness, well-being, and togetherness. Embrace this journey with an open heart, and you'll find that a simpler, more meaningful family life is well within reach.

Raising Minimalist Children

Introducing your children to minimalism can be both exciting and challenging. The journey often starts with the parents' own commitment to a simpler life, creating a home environment that prioritizes experiences and relationships over material possessions. By being consistent and leading by example, you can help your children embrace minimalism organically and joyfully.

One of the first steps in raising minimalist children is to engage them in conversations about values. Discuss what truly matters in life, such as spending quality time together, exploring nature, and giving back to the community. These conversations will provide a strong foundation for them to understand that happiness doesn't come from accumulating things but from meaningful experiences and connections.

It's important to include children in the decluttering process. Begin with their play areas and rooms, inviting them to sort through their toys and clothes. This activity can be a teachable moment; explain that donating or passing on items can make another child happy. Celebrate these decisions, making them feel proud of their choices.

Encouragement and praise can go a long way in reinforcing minimalist behaviors. When your child lets go of an item they no longer need or chooses an experience over a new toy, acknowledge their decision positively. Not only does this build their confidence, but it also strengthens their internal motivation to maintain a minimalist mindset.

Being selective about what enters your home is crucial. Limit toys and gifts to those that are high-quality, durable, and encourage creativity. Additionally, teach your children the value of waiting and saving for something they truly want instead of opting for instant gratification. This patience can instill a sense of appreciation and understanding of the value of things.

Another strategy is to incorporate minimalism into holidays and celebrations. Instead of focusing on material gifts, create memorable traditions like special family outings, cooking together, or volunteering. These practices can help children associate happiness with shared moments rather than objects.

In our digital age, managing screen time is a significant part of raising minimalist children. Encourage activities that involve physical movement, creativity, and interaction with the natural world. Set clear boundaries for screen use and model these habits yourself. Reflect on their digital consumption and talk about the importance of real-life connections and offline hobbies.

Self-care is a crucial aspect of minimalism that can be easily taught to children. Encourage them to engage in mindfulness practices such as simple meditation, reading, or just taking a quiet moment to reflect. These habits can help them develop emotional clarity and resilience.

Patience and consistency are key. Children may initially resist these changes, but over time, they can adapt and come to appreciate the minimalist lifestyle. Make minimalism a fun and rewarding process, looking for opportunities to learn and grow together.

Remember that the goal isn't perfection but progress. Raising minimalist children is about showing them the joys of a simpler life and helping them discover that the things that truly matter can't be bought. Your efforts will lay a strong foundation for them to lead a life filled with passion, purpose, and genuine happiness.

Chapter 9: Sustainable Living

Transitioning to a sustainable lifestyle isn't just about protecting the planet; it's about creating a life that resonates with simplicity and meaning. Embracing eco-friendly choices can seem daunting, but it's manageable and rewarding once you begin. Start by considering the everyday items you use: how can you reduce waste and choose more sustainable alternatives? From opting for reusable bags to choosing energy-efficient appliances, each small step contributes to a larger impact. Reducing your carbon footprint through mindful consumption, conscientious recycling, and supporting local businesses creates a positive ripple effect. This journey aligns perfectly with the minimalist philosophy, as it encourages you to value quality over quantity, fostering deeper connections with your environment and community. Sustainable living invites us to reassess our relationship with the world around us, ultimately leading to a more harmonious and fulfilling existence.

Eco-Friendly Choices

The journey to sustainable living isn't just about reducing clutter and focusing on what truly matters—it's about making choices that are kind to the planet. Eco-friendly choices are an essential part of this journey, and they tie naturally into the minimalist ethos. By making decisions that support the health of our environment, we also enhance our well-being. There's an empowering simplicity in knowing that our lifestyle choices make a positive impact, both on a personal scale and globally.

CHAPTER 9: SUSTAINABLE LIVING

One of the fundamental ways to begin embracing an eco-friendly lifestyle is to evaluate our consumption habits. Consider adopting a mindset where you "reduce, reuse, and recycle." Reducing waste means being mindful of what you bring into your home. Ask yourself whether each new item is truly necessary. Reusing items can be approached creatively—think about how everyday objects might serve multiple purposes before you discard or replace them. Recycling is the last resort; it's crucial to ensure that items are disposed of in ways that they'll be repurposed and kept out of landfills as long as possible.

Another significant shift can be made in our approach to food. Opting for a more plant-based diet can reduce your carbon footprint significantly. Agriculture, particularly meat production, has a profound impact on the environment. Incorporating more vegetables, fruits, legumes, and grains not only benefits your health but also reduces the demand for resource-intensive animal farming. Furthermore, consider buying local and seasonal produce. Supporting local farmers ensures you're getting fresh, nutrient-rich foods while reducing the environmental toll associated with transporting goods over long distances.

Moreover, mindful water use is a pivotal part of living sustainably. Simple changes, such as fixing leaks, taking shorter showers, and installing water-efficient fixtures, can lead to substantial water savings. Collecting rainwater for gardening or using greywater systems can also make a notable difference. Remember, every drop counts.

Energy consumption is another critical area where eco-friendly choices can be exercised. Switch to energy-efficient appliances and lighting. LED bulbs, for instance, use less energy and last significantly longer than traditional incandescent bulbs. Additionally, be conscious about unplugging devices and turning off lights when they're not needed. Consider transitioning to renewable energy sources if feasible; solar panels, for example, can significantly reduce your home's carbon footprint over time.

Transportation is another major factor in environmental impact. If possible, opt for walking, cycling, or public transportation over personal vehicle usage. Carpooling is another excellent option for reducing the number of vehicles on the road. For those who need to drive, consider fuel-efficient or hybrid vehicles that use less gasoline and emit fewer pollutants. As electric vehicle technology becomes more advanced and accessible, they represent the future of eco-friendly transportation options.

Additionally, consider your home's overall environmental footprint. Insulating your home properly can reduce the need for excessive heating and cooling, resulting in lower energy use. Look into sustainable building materials for renovations, which can minimize the environmental damage caused by construction. Using non-toxic paints and sustainable materials like bamboo or reclaimed wood not only lessens your impact but also creates a healthier living space.

Fashion is another area ripe for sustainable change. Fast fashion's allure comes with substantial environmental and social costs. Instead of frequently buying cheap, trendy items, focus on purchasing high-quality, timeless pieces that are versatile and durable. Whenever possible, buy second-hand or swap clothing with friends to extend the life of garments. Supporting brands that prioritize ethical and eco-friendly production practices also makes a significant difference.

The intersection of minimalism and eco-friendly living encourages us to think critically about our possessions and habits, fostering a deeper appreciation for fewer, better things. By adopting sustainable choices, we not only declutter our physical surroundings but also contribute positively to the world around us. The result is a lifestyle that's richer in experience, connection, and purpose.

Let's not forget the importance of community in making these changes. Sharing resources—whether it's tools, knowledge, or vehicles—can significantly reduce waste. Joining or forming community organizations dedicated to environmental issues can amplify your impact. Community gardens, for instance, not only provide fresh produce but also foster a sense of togetherness and shared purpose.

Educating yourself and others about the reasons for and benefits of eco-friendly choices enriches the journey. Read extensively, follow thought leaders on sustainability, and engage in conversations with those around you. The more awareness spreads, the more impactful these choices become.

Don't underestimate the power of small actions. Switching to reusable shopping bags, water bottles, and coffee cups can collectively have a profound environmental impact. Switching to eco-friendly cleaners and personal care products reduces your exposure to harmful chemicals and reduces pollutant runoff into waterways.

In conclusion, the shift towards eco-friendly living integrated into a minimalist lifestyle doesn't happen overnight. It's a continuous process of learning and adapting. Embrace the journey with patience and compassion for yourself and those around you. Celebrate each small victory, knowing that together, these efforts accumulate into significant positive change. Sustainable living is a rewarding path, filled with opportunities to enhance our lives and protect the world we are privileged to inhabit.

Reducing Carbon Footprint

In today's fast-paced world, reducing our carbon footprint is more than just a trend; it's a responsibility. The choices we make every day, from the food we eat to the way we travel, all contribute to our individual carbon footprints. If we aim to live more sustainably, it's essential to understand how our actions impact the environment and what changes we can make to reduce our carbon emissions.

One of the most impactful steps we can take is to reduce energy consumption in our homes. Energy-efficient appliances may require an initial investment, but they pay off in the long run, both financially and environmentally. Switch to LED bulbs, unplug electronics when they are not in use, and consider investing in smart home systems that optimize energy usage.

Another simple yet powerful change is to reduce water usage. Fixing leaks promptly, using low-flow showerheads, and only running dishwashers and washing machines with full loads can significantly cut down on water waste. Remember, conserving water also means conserving the energy required to pump, heat, and treat water.

When it comes to transportation, the options for reducing carbon emissions are plentiful and varied. Walking, cycling, and public transportation are fantastic ways to cut down on fossil fuel consumption. For those who require a car, carpooling or opting for hybrid or electric vehicles can make a significant difference. Moreover, regular maintenance of your vehicle ensures it runs efficiently, further reducing emissions.

Dietary choices also play a crucial role in reducing our carbon footprint. Consuming more plant-based meals can significantly reduce greenhouse gas emissions associated with meat production. You don't need to become vegan overnight, but incorporating "meatless Mondays" or gradually increasing plant-based meals can make a noticeable impact. Additionally, supporting local farmers and eating seasonally can reduce the carbon emissions associated with food transportation and storage.

Waste management is another critical area to focus on. Reducing, reusing, and recycling should be second nature to anyone aiming to live sustainably. Opt for products with minimal packaging, bring reusable bags when shopping, and try to buy in bulk to cut down on individual packaging waste. Composting organic waste not only reduces landfill contributions but also enriches soil, benefiting gardens and reducing the need for chemical fertilizers.

Shopping habits greatly influence our carbon footprint. Fast fashion and the cycle of constantly buying new items, especially clothing, contribute significantly to environmental degradation. Instead, consider investing in high-quality, durable items that will last longer. Thrift stores are a treasure trove of sustainable fashion, often offering unique and high-quality pieces without the environmental cost of producing new items. Moreover, participate in clothing swaps with friends or community members to refresh your wardrobe in an eco-friendly way.

Travel is another area where we can make substantial improvements. While flying is sometimes unavoidable, it's one of the largest contributors to an individual's carbon footprint. Whenever possible, choose trains or buses for short to medium distances. If flying is necessary, consider purchasing carbon offsets, which fund projects aimed at reducing greenhouse gas emissions. Planning for longer vacations rather than frequent short trips can also reduce overall air travel frequency and thus lower your carbon footprint.

Home improvements and renovations offer another significant opportunity to reduce your carbon footprint. Insulating your home properly, using eco-friendly and sustainable materials for renovations, and installing solar panels are all effective methods. Proper insulation keeps your home warm in winter and cool in summer, reducing the need for excessive heating and air conditioning. Solar panels, while initially expensive, eventually pay for themselves by dramatically lowering energy bills and reducing reliance on non-renewable energy sources.

Lastly, education and advocacy can amplify your impact. Share your knowledge and habits with friends, family, and your community. Join local environmental groups and participate in initiatives aimed at promoting sustainable practices. Advocacy can also mean supporting policies and leaders committed to environmental sustainability. Your voice and vote can contribute to broader changes that benefit the planet.

Reducing your carbon footprint is a journey, not a destination. It's about making better, more informed choices consistently and inspiring others to do the same. By adopting a minimalist mindset and focusing on what truly matters, we naturally gravitate towards a more sustainable lifestyle. Every step, big or small, counts towards a healthier planet and a simpler, more meaningful life.

Remember, it's not about achieving perfection but making consistent efforts to improve. Embrace the journey, celebrate your progress, and recognize that your actions, combined with those of many others, have the power to create significant positive change.

Chapter 10: Minimalism in Work and Productivity

In today's fast-paced world, the principles of minimalism can be a game changer for boosting work and productivity. By simplifying task management and focusing on what truly matters, we free ourselves from the noise and chaos that often accompany our daily grind. Imagine a workspace that is both physically and mentally unburdened; it's not just about a clean desk but a clear head as well. The essence of minimalism in work lies in prioritizing key tasks and eliminating unnecessary distractions. It's about honing in on your goals with laser-like precision and creating systems that support rather than hinder your progress. This approach not only enhances efficiency but also fosters a sense of fulfillment and balance. By integrating minimalist practices into your work life, you'll find that you can achieve more by doing less, ultimately paving the way for sustained productivity and well-being.

Simplifying Task Management

Task management, when aligned with minimalistic principles, can become an empowering way to lead a more focused and rewarding professional life. Too often, our workday morphs into a chaotic rush of to-dos, reminders, and postponed activities. Imagine, instead, a streamlined approach where tasks are organized, prioritized, and accomplished with clarity. This isn't about doing less for the sake of it, but about ensuring that every task you undertake

CHAPTER 10: MINIMALISM IN WORK AND PRODUCTIVITY

carries genuine value.

To start simplifying task management, let's consider the tools you use. It's easy to get overwhelmed with a myriad of productivity apps and planners, but minimalism advocates for the principle of "less is more." Select tools that work effortlessly for you—a simple notebook, a concise digital planner, or even a bullet journal. The focus should be on utility and ease, reducing the mental load generated by having to juggle multiple systems. Overcomplicating your task management means you're more likely to abandon it when life gets busy.

Once you've narrowed down your tools, it's important to capture and prioritize your tasks effectively. Start each day by listing out your top three most critical tasks. This doesn't mean you won't do more than three, but these should be the tasks that will significantly impact your day or contribute toward your long-term goals. Doing this fosters a sense of achievement and keeps your mind free from the clutter of less essential duties. It's an approach reminiscent of the Pareto Principle, where 20% of your efforts produce 80% of your results.

Consider also the practice of time blocking. Allocate specific chunks of time to particular tasks without distraction. Time blocking can help maintain focused energy on what truly matters. For instance, block an hour in the morning to handle emails, then dedicate the next two hours to project work. After that, you might allocate time to meetings or creative brainstorming. Keeping these blocks clear and adhering to them can prevent the scattershot approach that leaves tasks half-finished and energy depleted.

It's vital to cultivate the habit of single-tasking as opposed to multitasking. Multitasking might seem like a way to get more done, but studies have shown it actually reduces productivity and increases stress. When you're working on a task, give it your full attention. This single-minded focus not only completes tasks more efficiently but also ensures that you're delivering quality results, thus trimming down the time needed for corrections or revisions later.

Decluttering your task list itself can be incredibly impactful. Regularly review your tasks to eliminate or delegate those that aren't aligned with your objectives or values. This strategy can parallel the decluttering of physical spaces. By removing the unnecessary and the non-essential, you leave room for what truly matters. You can also categorize tasks into what's urgent, important, and may be ignored. A simple two-column matrix (urgent-important and urgent-trivial) might be all you need to sift the wheat from the chaff.

A crucial aspect of simplifying task management is learning to set boundaries and say no. It's tempting to agree to every request, but that leads to overcommitment and stress. Every time you accept a new task, ensure it aligns with your priorities. If it doesn't fit, have the confidence to decline politely. Setting boundaries is not about being uncooperative, but about safeguarding your time and energy for what truly matters. This empowers you to work more effectively and with greater satisfaction, knowing that your efforts are aligned with your goals.

Incorporate regular breaks and downtime into your schedule. The Pomodoro Technique is a helpful tool—work for a solid 25 minutes, then take a 5-minute break. After four cycles, take a longer break. This method keeps your mind fresh and prevents burnout. By factoring rest into your schedule, you're able to maintain high productivity levels without draining yourself.

Another strategy is to use themes for different days of the week. For instance, dedicate Mondays to planning and strategic thinking, Tuesdays to client meetings, Wednesdays to project work, and so on. This thematic approach allows for a deep dive into related tasks, promoting a flow state where productivity can flourish. It's a subtle but powerful way to bring order and consistency to your workweek.

Equally important is the habit of reflection and adjustment. At the end of each week, review what was accomplished and identify what could be improved. This practice not only celebrates your achievements but also highlights areas where tweaks are needed, ensuring your task management system evolves with your changing needs and priorities.

Effective communication plays a role in simplifying task management. Clearly articulate your goals and expectations with your team to minimize misunderstandings and redundancy. When everyone knows their roles and responsibilities, tasks are completed more efficiently, and there's less need

CHAPTER 10: MINIMALISM IN WORK AND PRODUCTIVITY

for constant oversight or correction.

If you're working on larger projects, break them down into smaller, manageable tasks. This chunking method makes big goals seem less daunting and provides a steady stream of achievable milestones. Celebrate these small wins to maintain motivation and recognize progress. This approach mirrors the minimalist philosophy of taking deliberate, thoughtful actions that contribute to the overall goal without getting overwhelmed by the bigger picture.

Mind your environment as well. A clutter-free workspace can help maintain a clear mind and foster productivity. Keep your desk tidy, but also personalize it with items that inspire you. A clean and organized environment can serve as a physical manifestation of the clarity and focus you aspire to in your task management.

Lastly, embrace the principle of ongoing simplification. Minimalism in task management is not a one-time effort but a continual practice of assessing and refining how you approach your work. Regularly revisit your strategies, tools, and methods to ensure they still serve you effectively. Be open to letting go of what's no longer beneficial and adopting new practices that support your evolving goals.

By simplifying task management through these mindful strategies, you're not just clearing a path to increased productivity. You're creating a space where meaningful work can flourish, and stress can be minimized. Embracing minimalism in your professional life paves the way for a more intentional, satisfying journey where every task you undertake genuinely counts.

Focusing on What Matters

In a world that's constantly demanding our attention, being intentional about what we focus on can be a game-changer. When we talk about "Focusing on What Matters," we're not just talking about making to-do lists or prioritizing tasks. We're talking about a fundamental shift in how you approach your work and your life. It's about letting go of the non-essentials and honing in on the activities and goals that truly align with your values and aspirations.

One of the key principles of minimalism in work and productivity is the idea that less is more. It's easy to get caught up in the whirlwind of meetings, emails, endless to-dos, and multitasking. But how much of that is actually contributing to meaningful progress? Probably not as much as you think. The first step towards focusing on what matters is to identify what doesn't. This means ruthlessly eliminating distractions and commitments that drain your time and energy without offering significant returns.

Think about the 80/20 rule, also known as the Pareto Principle. This principle suggests that roughly 80% of results come from 20% of efforts. By identifying the 20% of tasks that bring the most value, you can focus your time and energy more effectively. This doesn't mean neglecting all responsibilities but strategically deciding where to invest your efforts for maximum impact.

Prioritization is crucial. Start by listing all your tasks and responsibilities. Then, categorize them into different levels of importance and urgency. Which tasks will drive the most significant progress towards your goals? Which ones align with your long-term vision? Allocate your time accordingly, giving precedence to high-impact activities.

It's equally important to recognize the power of saying "no." By declining tasks and projects that don't align with your priorities, you create space for what truly matters. Saying no is not about being difficult or uncooperative; it's about setting boundaries to protect your focus and energy. Remember, every time you say yes to something unimportant, you are saying no to something that could be genuinely transformative.

Embracing monotasking over multitasking is another pivotal element. While multitasking is often celebrated as a skill, numerous studies show it can severely affect your productivity and cognitive function. When you split your attention across multiple tasks, the quality of your work suffers, and it usually takes longer to complete. Concentrating on one task at a time lets you fully immerse yourself in it, leading to higher quality work and a greater sense of accomplishment.

Another effective strategy is time blocking. Allocate specific blocks of time for focused work on your most important tasks. During these periods, eliminate distractions—turn off notifications, set your phone to do not disturb, and avoid any non-critical meetings. This dedicated focus time can drastically

CHAPTER 10: MINIMALISM IN WORK AND PRODUCTIVITY

improve your productivity and help you maintain a state of flow, where you are fully engaged and working efficiently.

Regularly reviewing your goals and commitments is also essential. Set aside time each week or month to evaluate your progress and make adjustments as needed. Are your actions aligned with your goals? Have any new priorities emerged? This reflection period offers a chance to recalibrate and ensure you remain focused on what matters most.

Moreover, cultivating a minimalist mindset in your approach to work can transform how you perceive and handle tasks. Adopt the mantra "less but better." This means committing to fewer projects and tasks but doing each one exceptionally well. It's about depth over breadth and ensuring the quality of your work reflects your values and goals.

Effective delegation is another powerful tool. Recognize that you don't have to do everything yourself. Trusting others with tasks that don't need your unique skills frees you up to focus on where you can make the most impact. Delegation isn't about offloading work; it's about utilizing resources wisely to ensure that the most critical work gets the attention it needs.

Taking care of your mental and physical well-being ensures you have the energy and clarity to focus on what matters. Incorporate practices like meditation, mindfulness, and regular exercise into your routine. These activities clear your mind, reduce stress, and boost your overall productivity. A well-rested, calm mind is far more capable of discerning what's truly important.

You also must craft a workspace that fosters focus and minimizes distractions. A clutter-free, organized workspace can significantly enhance your ability to concentrate and think clearly. Keep only essential items on your desk and store other items neatly away. Your workspace should be a place that encourages focus and creativity, not chaos and distraction.

Remember, focusing on what matters isn't a one-time task; it's a continuous process. Life is dynamic, and so are your priorities. Regularly reassess what's important in your career and personal life. Adapt and make changes as necessary to ensure you remain focused on what truly brings value and joy to your life.

Adopting a minimalist approach to work and productivity isn't about doing less for the sake of less. It's about doing less to achieve more. By focusing on what really matters, you're not just improving your productivity; you're enriching your life with purpose and meaning. You're creating space for growth, creativity, and genuine fulfillment.

So, as you move forward, embrace this minimalist mindset. Be intentional about your focus. Make choices that align with your true values and goals. In doing so, you're not just working smarter—you're paving the way for a more fulfilling and meaningful life.

Chapter 11: The Art of Saying No

Mastering the art of saying no is essential if you want to lead a life that's both meaningful and free from unnecessary burdens. It's not just about turning others down; it's about creating space for what truly matters to you. By setting boundaries, you protect your energy and time, allowing you to invest in activities and relationships that align with your values. Embracing the power of no means understanding your limits and prioritizing self-care, thus crafting a more intentional and fulfilling way of living. Remember, saying no is a courageous act of self-respect and a pivotal step toward downsizing your life to upsize your happiness.

Setting Boundaries

Embracing minimalism means more than just decluttering your home and your mind. A crucial part of this journey is learning to set boundaries, both with others and yourself. It's about creating a protective barrier for your time, space, and energy, which are your most valuable resources.

Setting boundaries begins with a shift in mindset. You must recognize that it's not only okay but necessary to say "no" sometimes. This might be challenging, especially if you've always been a people-pleaser. However, imagine how much simpler and more meaningful your life can be when you're not bogged down by commitments that don't serve you.

One of the first steps to setting boundaries is to get clear on your values and priorities. When you understand what truly matters to you, it's easier to discern which requests align with your goals and which ones don't. This clarity is your compass. It guides you in making decisions that respect your time and energy.

For instance, think about the last social event you attended out of obligation rather than desire. How did you feel afterward? Likely exhausted and resentful. Now, imagine saying "no" and spending that time on an activity that rejuvenates you. Setting boundaries allows you to make these conscious choices that prioritize your well-being.

But how do we set these boundaries without feeling guilty? It's all about framing your decisions positively. Instead of focusing on the "no," think about what you're saying "yes" to. For example, turning down an unnecessary work meeting might mean freeing up time for a passion project or quality time with your family. When you view your boundaries as a way to protect what's important, it becomes easier to enforce them.

In the workplace, setting boundaries can be particularly tricky, especially in a culture that often equates busyness with productivity. However, saying "no" to excessive tasks and meetings that don't align with your core responsibilities can increase your efficiency and job satisfaction. It's about working smarter, not harder.

A practical approach here is to communicate your boundaries clearly and assertively. This doesn't mean being rude or uncooperative. Instead, it's about being honest and transparent about your limitations and priorities.

For example, practice saying, "I appreciate the opportunity, but I won't be able to take on this project as it would compromise my ability to complete my current tasks effectively." This kind of communication shows respect for your time and capabilities, and it can set a precedent that helps others respect your boundaries as well.

In personal relationships, setting boundaries can mean letting go of toxic behaviors and people who drain your energy. It might feel uncomfortable initially, as our social norms often push us to avoid confrontation. However, safeguarding your mental and emotional health is paramount.

Start with small steps, such as limiting how often you interact with someone who leaves you feeling depleted. Gradually, you can become more assertive, expressing your needs and expectations clearly. Over time, you'll find that healthy boundaries improve your relationships by fostering mutual respect.

Don't forget to set boundaries with yourself, too. Self-discipline is a cornerstone of minimalism. For example, if you know that starting your day with social media leaves you feeling distracted, set a boundary to check updates only during a specific time of the day. This small change can significantly impact your focus and productivity.

Additionally, setting financial boundaries is essential in a minimalist lifestyle. It's crucial to know when to say "no" to unnecessary purchases that clutter your home and life. One way to do this is by implementing a "24-hour rule" where you wait a day before making non-essential purchases. This time gap often reduces impulsive buying and helps you make mindful decisions.

Another aspect to consider is setting boundaries around your digital life. Limit your screen time, unsubscribe from distracting notifications, and curate your digital space to align with your minimalist values. By doing so, you free up not just physical and mental space but also the time to engage in activities that truly add value to your life.

Setting boundaries isn't a one-time act but an ongoing practice. As you grow and your priorities shift, you'll need to reassess and adjust your boundaries accordingly. This is a natural part of the process and a sign of your evolving understanding of what constitutes a fulfilling life.

The beauty of boundaries is that they empower you to live more authentically. They give you the permission to focus on what truly matters, making room for more joy and less stress. By aligning your external commitments with your internal values, you create a harmonious balance that simplifies your life and amplifies your happiness.

Remember, setting boundaries isn't about building walls; it's about prioritizing your well-being. It's a profound act of self-respect and a vital component of a minimalist lifestyle. When you master the art of saying "no," you open the door to a more intentional, meaningful life. And isn't that what minimalism is all about?

Prioritizing Self-C Care

Saying no is an art, and at its very heart lies the fundamental principle of prioritizing self-care. We live in a society often driven by the word "yes," with a persistent pressure to accommodate, to please, and to engage. While accommodating others can be virtuous, an inability to say no can lead to exhaustion, burnout, and ultimately, a disconnection from oneself. This is why making self-care a priority is not just beneficial, but necessary.

It's easy to fall into the trap of thinking self-care is a luxury or an act of selfishness. However, self-care is, in fact, a vital act of self-respect and preservation. When you prioritize self-care, you're not just pampering yourself; you're maintaining the engine that drives every aspect of your life. Your physical health, mental clarity, emotional stability, and even your ability to nurture relationships depend on how well you take care of yourself. By learning to say no to things that deplete your energy, you can say yes to those that nourish and rejuvenate you.

Consider how often you overextend yourself, agreeing to commitments that leave you feeling stretched thin. Always saying yes can result in a to-do list perpetually brimming with tasks you perform half-heartedly. The stress that follows impacts your well-being, slowly eroding the joy and enthusiasm you might have had initially. In contrast, saying no can create space for activities and experiences that align with your true values and passions.

One fundamental aspect of self-care involves understanding your own boundaries. Knowing your limits allows you to protect your time and energy more effectively. It's about recognizing what drains you and what fills you up. For example, if you're consistently saying yes to late-night social gatherings despite needing a good night's sleep to function well, you're not aligning your actions with your foundational needs. Being aware of such discrepancies is the first step toward reshaping your habits and prioritizing your well-being.

Setting boundaries is an act of courage and an affirmation of your priorities. It's allowing yourself to honor commitments to your well-being by prioritizing what truly matters. Whether it's a few minutes of meditation, a walk in nature, or simply saying no to an extra work project, these small acts accumulate over

CHAPTER 11: THE ART OF SAYING NO

time, leading to a substantial improvement in your quality of life.

Creating a sustainable self-care routine requires a shift in mindset. Instead of viewing self-care as an indulgence, consider it a discipline—one that's essential for your overall health and happiness. Regularly checking in with yourself to gauge your mental, emotional, and physical state can be incredibly insightful. These self-check-ins can guide you in making necessary adjustments, whether that means taking a break, seeking support, or altering your commitments.

Additionally, self-care isn't limited to solitary activities or alone time. It also encompasses relationships and social interactions that uplift and support you. Surrounding yourself with individuals who respect your boundaries and understand your need for self-care can create a nurturing environment that significantly enhances your well-being. It might mean reevaluating relationships that drain your energy and instead fostering those that contribute to your growth and happiness.

In the workplace, prioritizing self-care can be challenging but is equally important. Balancing professional responsibilities with personal needs is crucial for preventing burnout. Learning to say no to extra assignments or unrealistic deadlines can help you maintain this balance. Be honest with your colleagues or supervisor about your workload and limits. Most employers appreciate transparency and respect employees who manage their time effectively.

Moreover, consider integrating mindfulness practices into your work routine. Short breaks for deep breathing, walking, or even a few moments of silence can make a significant difference in how you feel throughout the day. Such practices can help alleviate stress and improve concentration, enabling you to perform more effectively and sustainably.

Another crucial aspect to consider is how digital life impacts your self-care. The omnipresence of technology can be a source of stress and distraction. Setting boundaries with your digital devices, such as turning off notifications during certain times, designating tech-free zones, or banning digital devices from the bedroom, can be profound acts of self-care. These steps can reduce digital overload and help you stay present in your offline life.

Incorporating self-care into your daily routine doesn't have to be overwhelming. It can be as simple as starting your day with a few moments of gratitude, scheduling regular downtime, or enjoying nourishing meals. The key is to make these practices consistent. Over time, these small shifts can lead to significant improvements in your overall health and happiness.

Ultimately, the art of saying no is deeply intertwined with the practice of self-care. By adopting this practice, you consciously decide to place your well-being at the forefront. While it may require overcoming initial feelings of guilt or discomfort, remember that this is an act of self-love. Prioritizing self-care allows you to show up more fully in all other areas of your life. This simple yet powerful decision can set the stage for greater joy, fulfillment, and resilience.

So, embrace the discomfort and practice saying no when you need to. Honor your needs, set your boundaries, and cherish your moments of self-care. Doing so is not just an act of refusal, but a profound statement of your commitment to living a life that's fulfilling and sustainable. Prioritizing self-care empowers you to downsize the noise and demands of life, paving the way for true happiness and simplicity.

Chapter 12: Maintaining a Minimalist Lifestyle

Maintaining a minimalist lifestyle is about continual improvement and embracing change with open arms. It isn't a one-time project but an ongoing journey that weaves through every facet of life. Periodically reassess your possessions, relationships, and commitments to ensure they still serve your core values. Embrace new habits that further streamline your environment and mind. Welcome the ebb and flow of life's transitions, knowing that each shift offers an opportunity to refine what truly matters. Remember, minimalism is less about what you remove and more about what you add in terms of purpose and peace. Keep cultivating this lifestyle, and you'll find lasting happiness and clarity growing stronger with time.

Continual Improvement

Embracing a minimalist lifestyle is not a one-time event; it's a journey of continual improvement. It's about relentlessly fine-tuning your life to align with your core values and goals. Every day presents an opportunity to reassess what truly matters and adjust your surroundings, habits, and mindset accordingly. This constant evolution helps you to maintain the balance between simplicity and complexity in life, ensuring that you are always moving closer to a more meaningful, purpose-driven existence.

The concept of continual improvement in minimalism revolves around the principle of Kaizen, a Japanese term for "continuous improvement". Applying this principle means being open to small but consistent changes over time. Rather than adopting an all-or-nothing attitude, you focus on incremental adjustments that gradually lead to substantial benefits. These small changes can compound, leading to profound transformations in your lifestyle.

One practical approach to continual improvement is to conduct regular audits of your physical and digital spaces. Just as you initially decluttered your home or streamlined your digital life, periodic reviews ensure that you are not unknowingly accumulating items or data that don't serve your purpose. Set a schedule to revisit your decluttering decisions every few months, asking yourself if these items still add value to your life. If not, it's time to let them go.

Reflection is a key component of continual improvement. Allocate time each week to reflect on your minimalist journey. Consider what has worked well and what challenges you've faced. This self-reflection helps you identify areas for improvement and consolidate practices that have had a positive impact. Journaling can be a powerful tool in this process, as it allows you to document your thoughts and monitor your progress over time.

Habits play a crucial role in maintaining a minimalist lifestyle. Evaluate your daily routines and identify habits that may be leading to unnecessary complexity or clutter. Are you prone to impulse buying? Do you often sign up for subscriptions or services you don't need? By identifying these habits, you can take deliberate actions to change them, replacing them with more aligned and purposeful behaviors.

Mindfulness and minimalism go hand in hand. Practicing mindfulness helps you stay present and aware of your choices. Incorporate mindfulness techniques such as meditation or deep-breathing exercises into your daily routine. These practices enhance your ability to make intentional decisions rather than reacting to external pressures or emotional impulses. When you are more mindful, you are better equipped to recognize when something does not fit your minimalist lifestyle and make necessary adjustments.

Resilience is another important aspect of continual improvement. Life is unpredictable, and there will be moments when you face setbacks or challenges that threaten to disrupt your minimalist way of living. Developing resilience means being adaptable and using these challenges as opportunities for growth. When faced with obstacles, ask yourself what you can learn from the experience and how you can use it to further streamline and simplify your life.

Another key element is community. Engaging with like-minded individuals can provide you with support, inspiration, and new ideas for maintaining and enhancing your minimalist lifestyle. Join minimalist groups or online forums where you can share your experiences and learn from others. The collective wisdom of a community can be a valuable resource for continual improvement.

Continual improvement also involves reassessing your goals and aspirations. Over time, your values and priorities may shift. What was important to you a year ago might not hold the same significance today. Revisit your goals regularly and make adjustments to ensure they still align with your current values. This practice keeps your minimalist lifestyle dynamic and relevant to your present circumstances.

It's essential to celebrate your progress. Recognizing and appreciating the strides you've made reinforces your commitment to a minimalist lifestyle. Take time to celebrate the milestones, no matter how small. Recognizing your achievements helps to motivate you and maintains the momentum for continual improvement.

Finally, embrace the idea that perfection is not the goal. Minimalism is not about achieving a perfect state; it's about making choices that enhance your life and bring you joy. Understand that it's okay to have setbacks and that continual improvement is about progress, not perfection. This mindset allows you to approach your minimalist journey with grace and kindness towards yourself, making the process more sustainable and enjoyable.

In summary, continual improvement in maintaining a minimalist lifestyle is a lifelong commitment to reassessment, reflection, and mindful choices. By adopting a mindset of gradual, incremental change, you can consistently align your life more closely with your values and goals. Through regular audits, reflection, habit changes, resilience, community engagement, goal reassessment, and celebrating progress, you ensure that your minimalist lifestyle remains vibrant and meaningful. Remember, the journey is not about perfection but about creating a life of greater simplicity, purpose, and contentment.

Embracing Change

Maintaining a minimalist lifestyle requires more than the initial decluttering surge. It demands vigilance, awareness, and a willingness to evolve. At its core, minimalism isn't a one-time event, but a continuous journey that invites you to embrace change regularly. Change is an inherent part of life, and adopting a minimalist mindset helps you navigate these transitions gracefully.

Change can feel daunting at times. It often involves letting go of the familiar and stepping into the unknown. In the context of minimalism, embracing change means being open to reevaluating your possessions, habits, and even your mindset regularly. This ongoing assessment ensures that your life remains aligned with your core values and goals, providing clarity and focus in an ever-evolving world.

The first step in embracing change is cultivating a mindset that welcomes it. This involves recognizing that everything in life is temporary and that clinging to the past can hinder your growth. Let go of the desire for permanence and appreciate the beauty of the present moment. This shift in perspective allows you to see opportunities in change rather than obstacles.

Minimalism teaches us to prioritize experiences over possessions, and this philosophy can be a powerful tool in navigating change. When you're less attached to material items, you become more adaptable. Reducing your attachment to physical objects frees up mental and emotional space, making it easier to adjust to new circumstances. With fewer possessions to manage, you're more agile and capable of embracing life's twists and turns.

One practical way to embrace change in your minimalist journey is to practice regular decluttering. Set aside time every few months to reassess your belongings. Ask yourself whether each item still adds value to your life. If not, it's time to let it go. This practice not only keeps your living space clutter-free but also reinforces the habit of letting go, making it easier to navigate larger

CHAPTER 12: MAINTAINING A MINIMALIST LIFESTYLE

life changes.

Change isn't limited to physical possessions; it also extends to your habits and routines. Minimalism encourages intentional living, which often involves rethinking your daily habits. Are there activities or commitments that no longer serve you? Be willing to let go of routines that detract from your well-being and replace them with ones that contribute positively to your life. Simplifying your habits can lead to greater productivity and a more fulfilling daily existence.

Embracing change also means being open to new experiences and opportunities. Minimalism creates space for growth and exploration. When you're not weighed down by excess, you have the freedom to pursue new interests and passions. Say yes to opportunities that align with your values and bring joy and meaning to your life. This openness to new experiences can lead to personal growth and a deeper sense of fulfillment.

Another aspect of embracing change is learning to adapt to different life stages. Your needs and priorities will evolve as you move through different phases of life. Minimalism provides the flexibility to adjust your lifestyle accordingly. Whether you're starting a new job, moving to a new city, or expanding your family, a minimalist mindset allows you to navigate these transitions with ease and grace.

Resilience is a key component of embracing change. Building resilience involves developing the mental and emotional strength to handle life's ups and downs. Minimalism fosters resilience by helping you focus on what truly matters. When you're not distracted by excess, you can devote your energy to nurturing relationships, pursuing meaningful goals, and taking care of your well-being. This foundation of stability and clarity makes it easier to bounce back from setbacks and adapt to new circumstances.

It's also important to acknowledge the emotional aspect of change. Letting go, whether it's of possessions, habits, or even relationships, can evoke a range of emotions. Allow yourself to feel these emotions and process them. Practice self-compassion and understand that it's okay to feel sad, anxious, or uncertain during times of change. Embracing change with empathy for yourself makes the transition smoother and more manageable.

Minimalism can also extend to your mindset and inner world. Embracing change means being open to shifting your perspectives and beliefs. Regularly challenge your assumptions and be willing to see things from different viewpoints. This mental flexibility not only enhances your personal growth but also contributes to a more harmonious and understanding world.

Creating a support system can be invaluable when navigating change. Surround yourself with people who share your values and understand your minimalist lifestyle. Share your experiences and learn from others who have embraced change successfully. A supportive community can provide encouragement, inspiration, and practical advice, making the process of embracing change less intimidating.

Embracing change also involves celebrating your progress and acknowledging your achievements. Take time to reflect on how far you've come on your minimalist journey. Celebrate the small victories and milestones, whether it's decluttering a room, simplifying a routine, or adopting a new habit. Recognizing your accomplishments reinforces your commitment to minimalism and motivates you to continue embracing change.

In conclusion, embracing change is an essential part of maintaining a minimalist lifestyle. It requires a mindset that values growth, adaptability, and intentional living. By regularly reassessing your possessions, habits, and mindset, you ensure that your life remains aligned with your values and goals. Embrace change with openness and resilience, and you'll find that it leads to a simpler, more meaningful, and fulfilling life.

Remember, the journey of minimalism is ongoing. It's not about reaching a destination but about continuously evolving and refining your life to reflect what truly matters. Embrace the beauty of change, and you'll discover a deeper sense of clarity, purpose, and happiness.

Conclusion

As we reach the end of our journey together, consider the transformative possibilities that lie ahead. Embracing minimalism is not just about owning fewer items; it's about creating a more meaningful life filled with richer

CHAPTER 12: MAINTAINING A MINIMALIST LIFESTYLE

experiences and deeper connections. By shedding the excess that weighs us down, we open pathways to find peace, joy, and contentment in the simplicity of what truly matters.

The philosophy of minimalism, rooted in ancient teachings and revitalized in our modern era, offers an escape from the relentless consumerism that marks our times. Through each chapter, we've explored different facets of this lifestyle. By reducing stress and focusing on happiness, learning to declutter both our physical spaces and digital lives, and embarking on the journey to financial freedom, we have laid the groundwork for a more intentional existence. Maintaining this simplicity often means saying "no" more than "yes," and that's perfectly okay.

Reflect on the benefits you've gained from this guide. Perhaps stress has given way to moments of serenity, or financial pressures have eased as your priorities shifted from possessions to experiences. Maybe your living space feels more like a sanctuary, or your digital detox has granted more mental clarity. Whatever transformations you've experienced, recognize that these are the stepping stones to a more fulfilling life.

We also delved into how minimalism can transform not just individual lives but entire families. The powerful act of simplifying family life and instilling these values in our children sets the stage for future generations to live mindfully and purposefully. These are significant shifts that can make your home environment more harmonious and aligned with your core values.

Furthermore, minimalism encourages sustainable living and a reduced carbon footprint. Every decision to consume less or choose eco-friendly options contributes to the well-being of our planet. The impact of these choices reverberates far beyond our immediate surroundings, emphasizing that our minimalist journey is also a commitment to global sustainability.

The minimalist mindset is perhaps one of the most powerful tools we can develop. It involves cultivating mental and emotional clarity, often achieved through practices like meditation and mindfulness. By focusing on what truly matters, we can navigate life's complexities with a clearer, more focused mind. This mental shift is where the true essence of minimalism resides.

As you continue on your minimalist path, remember that this is not a static, one-time event but an ongoing practice of continual improvement and embracing change. It's about making conscious choices every day that align with your values and foster a simpler, more meaningful lifestyle. Change is the only constant, and in minimalism, each change brings us closer to a life of intentionality and fulfillment.

Finally, let's not forget the art of saying "no." Setting boundaries and prioritizing self-care are crucial for maintaining a minimalist lifestyle. It's about reclaiming your time and energy for the things and people that truly matter. By saying "no" to the non-essentials, you say "yes" to a life filled with purpose and satisfaction.

The journey toward minimalism is deeply personal and uniquely yours. While this book provides the principles and tools, the true magic happens when you apply these concepts in ways that resonate with your life. Take the ideas that work for you, adapt the ones that need tweaking, and create a minimalist journey that reflects your unique path.

As you move forward, carry with you the core philosophy that has been underscored in every chapter: less is more. It's not about deprivation but rather about enrichment. It's about making space for moments, experiences, and connections that add value to your life. Minimalism, at its heart, invites you to live with greater purpose and more profound joy.

Your minimalist journey doesn't end with this book. It's an ever-evolving practice of intentional living. As you continue to declutter, prioritize, and simplify, you'll find new depths of tranquility and purpose. Keep exploring, keep questioning, and keep refining what minimalism means to you.

In conclusion, the essence of minimalism is boiled down to one powerful truth: life is enriched, not by the things we accumulate, but by the experiences and relationships we cultivate. By embracing minimalism, you have embarked on an empowering journey of self-discovery and intentional living. May this path continue to bring you peace, happiness, and fulfillment.

Thank you for taking this journey. Remember, every step you take towards simplicity is a step towards a more meaningful and joyous life. You're not just downsizing your possessions; you're upsizing your happiness. Here's to a life well-lived, brimming with purpose and clarity.

CHAPTER 12: MAINTAINING A MINIMALIST LIFESTYLE

Minimalism Resources and Tools

Diving deeper into minimalism often requires practical tools and inspirational guides. These resources can help you maintain the momentum or get back on track if you stumble.

- **Books and Audiobooks** - There are countless books out there, but some stand out for their depth and clarity. Consider titles that have stood the test of time or have been recommended by fellow minimalists. Audiobooks can be a flexible option for busy lifestyles.
- **Podcasts** - Podcasts offer a rich source of inspiration and practical advice. They can be a great way to stay connected with like-minded individuals and keep your minimalist journey fresh and energized.
- **Websites and Blogs** - Numerous websites dive into various aspects of minimalism, from decluttering tips to sustainable living advice. Find a few that resonate with your values and subscribe to their updates.
- **Apps** - Dedicated apps can simplify tracking your minimalist progress, be it for budgeting, habit tracking, or digital decluttering. Look for apps that are user-friendly and align with your goals.

As you embrace minimalism, it's essential to remember that it's not about perfection. It's about progress and making intentional choices that reflect your values. Use these resources to enrich your journey and keep you grounded in your objectives.

Whatever stage you're in, know that every step you take towards a minimalist lifestyle is a step towards a more fulfilling and liberated existence. Keep refining, keep questioning, and most importantly, keep enjoying the process.

Minimalism Resources and Tools

Transitioning to a minimalist lifestyle can feel like an overwhelming journey, but the good news is that you're not alone. There's a wealth of resources and tools available to guide and support you on this path. Whether you're looking to declutter your physical space, streamline your digital life, or adopt a more sustainable lifestyle, the right resources can make all the difference. Let's explore some of the most effective tools and resources that can simplify your journey to minimalism.

Books are a timeless resource, offering in-depth insights and practical advice. Some of the most influential books in the realm of minimalism include "The Life-Changing Magic of Tidying Up" by Marie Kondo, which provides a detailed approach to decluttering. "Digital Minimalism" by Cal Newport is essential for those aiming to simplify their digital lives. These books not only offer practical steps but also deeply connect with the reader on an emotional level, motivating change from within.

In addition to books, there are a variety of online platforms and websites dedicated to minimalism. Websites like The Minimalists, Becoming Minimalist, and Zen Habits offer articles, podcasts, and community forums where you can find support and encouragement. These platforms often feature testimonials and stories from individuals who have successfully embraced minimalism, providing you with real-life inspiration and practical tips.

Apps can play a crucial role in your minimalist journey. For managing physical clutter, apps like Sortly help you catalog and track items, making it easier to decide what to keep and what to let go. For digital minimalism, apps like Freedom and Forest help you stay focused by blocking distracting websites and encouraging productive habits. Budgeting apps like YNAB (You Need A Budget) can assist you in achieving financial freedom, a key component of minimalist living.

Communities and support groups, both online and offline, can offer invaluable support. Online forums like Reddit's r/minimalism provide a space for like-minded individuals to share tips, ask questions, and offer mutual encouragement. Local meetup groups and workshops can also provide face-to-face interaction and foster a sense of community, helping you stay committed to your minimalist goals.

Videos and documentaries can be incredibly motivating. Films such as "Minimalism: A Documentary About the Important Things" explore the lives of individuals who have adopted minimalism and highlight the benefits of living with less. YouTube channels like Matt D'Avella and Pick Up Limes offer regular content on living a minimalist lifestyle, from decluttering tips to mindful living advice.

Printable worksheets and planners can be very effective tools. These resources often include checklists for decluttering, goal-setting templates, and habit trackers. They provide a tangible way to mark your progress and stay organized. Websites like Etsy offer a variety of minimalist printables that you can download and use immediately.

While it's easy to get caught up in acquiring new tools and resources, it's essential to remember the core principle of minimalism: less is more. Start by identifying the resources that resonate most with you and gradually incorporate them into your life. The goal is to simplify, not overwhelm, so choose wisely.

Many minimalists find that mindfulness practices, such as meditation and journaling, are invaluable tools. These practices help cultivate awareness and intentionality, allowing you to focus on what truly matters. Apps like Headspace and Calm offer guided meditations specifically designed to support a minimalist mindset.

Workshops and retreats focused on minimalism provide immersive experiences that can accelerate your transformation. These events often combine practical activities, like decluttering sessions, with reflective exercises, such as mindfulness meditation. Participants report feeling more motivated and equipped to maintain their minimalist lifestyle after attending these immersive experiences.

Remember, the journey to minimalism is unique for everyone. What works for one person may not work for another. Experiment with different tools and resources, and be patient with yourself as you find what works best for you. The ultimate goal is to create a life that aligns with your values and brings you joy, and these resources are here to support you every step of the way.

Printed in Dunstable, United Kingdom